C000245802

American Trans Air TriStar 1 N186AT after push-back at Gatwick in September 1996. This aircraft made its maiden flight on 12 April 1974 and was delivered to Delta Air Lines as N706DA on 2 May. It was acquired by ATA on 15 January 1985. *Nick Granger*

Modern Civil Aircraft: 8
LOCKHEED TRISTAR
Philip Birtles

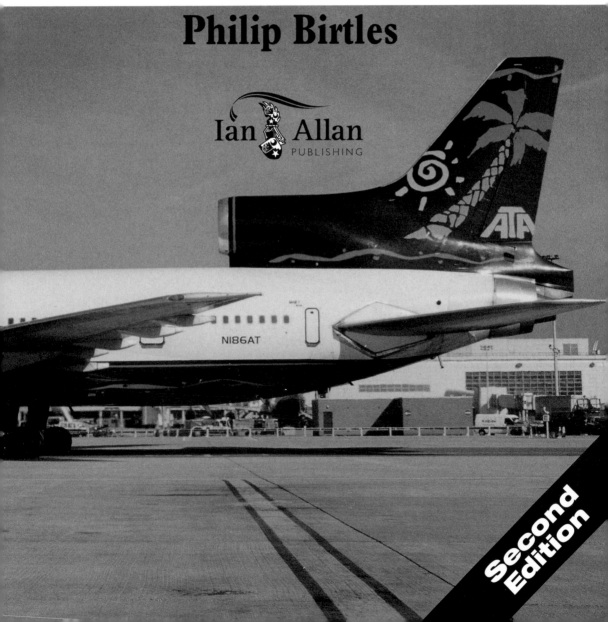

Ian Allan
PUBLISHING

Second Edition

Contents

All uncredited photographs courtesy of Lockheed California Co

First published 1989
Second edition 1999

ISBN 0 7110 2666 1

Published by Ian Allan Publishing

an imprint of Ian Allan Publishing Ltd, Terminal House, Shepperton, Surrey TW17 8AS.
Printed by Ian Allan Printing Ltd, Riverdene Business Park, Hersham, Surrey KT12 4RG.

Code: 9907/A2

Below:
A Canadian TriStar charter operator is Royal which was started in 1992 and operates three TriStars. TriStar 100 C-FTNI was originally with Air Canada, which flew its last service with this aircraft in October 1990. *Royal*

Author's Note

The Lockheed L-1011 TriStar has proved to be an interesting subject to research. The financial problems, technological advances, 'The Ghost of Flight 401', in addition to all the other features, provided interesting and varied material.

Although much of the research is a solitary activity, unselfish help was provided by Eric Schulzinger of the Lockheed California Co, Capt Terry Lakin, Flight Manager (Technical) TriStar with British Airways, the staff of Marshall Engineering of Cambridge, the Public Relations staff of the Ministry of Defence as well as RAF Strike Command and No 216 Squadron RAF at Brize Norton. My thanks to all these people, and especially to my wife, Martha, for her assistance and constructive critique.

Philip J. Birtles
Stevenage

Front cover:
All-Nippon Airways TriStar. *Robbie Shaw*

1 Evolution

Lockheed was an established commercial airliner manufacturer to the world's airlines after World War 2, as one of the 'Big Three' aerospace companies on the West Coast of the USA; Boeing and Douglas were the other two. Lockheed had produced the Constellation, later developed into the Starliner, while Douglas offered the DC-6 and DC-7 family and Boeing the Stratocruiser. When commercial air transport made the major jump into the jet age, Lockheed opted for the more economic prop-jet Electra, whereas Boeing and Douglas developed pure jet aircraft for the longer-range routes. While the turbo-prop was more economical for medium and short range operations, the major world markets developed with the long-range pure jet aircraft, allowing their eventual evolution into cost-effective transportation on all except the commuter and local airline operations.

Therefore, to catch up with civil jet airliner technology, Lockheed needed to be involved in a modern generation programme, or it would lose out on another major step which would almost certainly preclude a later re-entry into the commercial field.

In the early 1960s, two major civil airliner programmes were studied at Burbank in California. The first of these, starting in 1963, was the design in competition with Boeing of a proposed US supersonic transport (SST), funded by the US Government. Lockheed proposed a fixed wing delta design, but on 31 December 1966, this was rejected in favour of the variable geometry Boeing project. Later the Boeing design failed, on subsequent analysis, to meet the airline payload/range requirements and Boeing had to change to a fixed delta layout similar to the Lockheed proposal. In any event, the US SST was cancelled as being far too costly. The second programme was studies of the Giant C-5A military transport as a commercial aircraft, which were rejected.

Below:
The Lockheed Electra was not a commercial success due to competition from the jet airliners. A total of 170 were built and N1882 was the second aircraft used for trials and development. The Electra was later developed into the highly successful Orion maritime patrol aircraft.

During the early studies for the P-3C Orion long-range patrol aircraft for the US Navy based on the prop-jet Electra, the first seeds of a possible future commercial jet airliner were sown. During the preliminary design work, two-, three- and four-jet engine layouts were studied, but with typical navy-type long, thin fuselage and big wings giving long endurance. One of the twin-engined designs showed a great deal of promise, but was rejected by the US Navy due to its lack of enthusiasm for long missions over water on only two engines. Despite the rejection, the aircraft still looked reasonable, and thoughts began to turn towards a commercial design. With the capacity of the fuselage increased to carry a large number of passengers, it was studied by the Navy P-3C team in their spare time, despite the heavy workload. The result was a high-wing, big twin-fan engined aircraft, with the engines hung on underwing pods. The fuselage was oval shaped, wider than it was high, giving a passenger cabin capacity of 250 persons with a twin aisle layout. Weight and performance was briefly checked on a wind tunnel model, but pressure of work on the Orion took over and the schemes for the airliner were shelved.

In the autumn of 1966, a few months before the rejection of the Lockheed SST, American Airlines produced an outline specification for a large capacity, short to medium haul transport powered by the new technology large turbo-fan engines then becoming available. Lockheed decided to use this requirement as their basis for re-entering the commercial jet airliner field, although there was a direct competitor in the form of the McDonnell Douglas DC-10. Despite Lockheed's excellent relations with American Airlines, it became the first customer for the DC-10 on 19 February 1968, making it even more important for Lockheed to gain sufficient launch orders.

Before American Airlines' choice of the DC-10, Lockheed worked closely with the airline to define the design of its airbus. The requirement was for a 300-passenger aircraft with a similar performance to the Boeing 727, but a much better economy. American Airlines required a one-stop transcontinental range of 2,130 miles, while some of the other potential customers regarded non-stop transcontinental range as essential. A Mach 0.8 cruise and operations from a 9,000ft runway on a hot day were specified.

Although the American Airlines requirement was intitially no more than a five-page typed document, it defined a very restrictive requirement. The ultimate aim was to carry a maximum number of people at a minimum cost per seat/mile. This apparently meant a big twin-engined aircraft, similar in many ways to the earlier shelved ex-Navy design. The constraints came with the American Airlines investment in La Guardia, the downtown airport for New York City. The terminal had certain geometric constraints, which included the layout of the satellites and the turning areas, restricting the overall length. One of the runways was extended out over the bay on piers which at that time restricted gross weight on that portion to 270,000lb, but the piers have since been strengthened. The earlier schemes were pulled out and studied as a likely basis for the future airbus.

A primary design group was set up from the middle of 1966 and for six months a detailed exploration was made of the twin-engined aircraft. The aircraft was to be a wide-bodied aircraft between the size of the huge Boeing 747 and the smaller Boeing 707 or Douglas DC-8 first generation jet liners. With the loss of the SST programme by Lockheed in late December 1966, there were suddenly about 1,200 surplus engineers available. While some were temporarily laid off, many others were transferred on to the airbus project allowing it to go ahead with top priority.

As contacts grew with the major US domestic airlines, towards the end of 1966, a number of major objectives and requirements had been defined. Passenger comfort and appeal needed to be improved over the existing narrow-bodied jet airliners, while carrying double the payload on short to medium routes. Higher cruising speeds were required while using existing airport facilities. Higher utilisation needed to be achieved through faster turnround, and reliabilty needed to be improved, allied to design for ease of maintenance. Lower operating costs, lower noise levels and an automatic landing capability were all required to provide a more reliable operation and a better return on the initial capital investment in the aircraft. All this was required by the early 1970s, to be followed by a family of models extending the investment over longer business spans by broadening the scope of operations while retaining commonality in spares, maintenance, ground handling and training.

While establishing a design which would meet these basic requirements and achieve the necessary performance, the Lockheed design office evaluated 66 different configurations on a computer, leading to a basic layout in the early months of 1967. This was defined as the CL-1011-28, a wide-bodied, low- to mid-wing airframe with two engines located in underwing pods. With a gross design weight of 300,000lb, it would carry 250 passengers up to 1,600 miles. Wing span was 155ft and overall length 162ft. Alternative three-engined layouts were also studied under the designations CL-1011-30, -31,

-32, and -33, but the economics of the twin-engined version appeared much more promising.

Despite the prime interest by American Airlines, it was prudent to find out the requirements of other major carriers to achieve a broader basic design configuration. For example, Eastern Airlines was not happy with a twin-jet because its longest nonstop route was the 1,800 miles from New York to San Juan, much over water. There was a preference for a tri-jet with a 1,800-mile range. The wide-bodied high density fuselage was, however, an attraction. Trans World Airways (TWA) was also interested, as although it was just taking delivery of the 747s, the aircraft was too large and uneconomic for its domestic routes, especially Chicago to Los Angeles, and Kansas City or St Louis to the West Coast destinations. A 250-300 seat wide-bodied jet would be ideal, but TWA did not like the twin-jet idea, in case of engine failure over the Rockies. A single-engined diversion would require an engine of around 55,000lb thrust, and none of that power existed at that time. There was therefore a gradual leaning towards a tri-jet.

As the discussions with the operators continued during 1967, it became very clear that a nonstop US transcontinental range was desired and by September, the airlines were being offered the L-1011-365 with a gross weight of 320,000lb and a capacity of 227 passengers. A third engine had been added to the rear fuselage, with the air intake in the base of the fin leading edge. The power of the engines was to be about 35,000lb thrust each. At that time, it was felt that the ranges involved would not be acceptable for a twin-jet, and a tri-jet would improve operational flexibility on long routes over water. It would have fewer restrictions in poor visibility take-offs and landing, improved performance and security

in the event of an engine failure, and the ability to perform ferry fights on two engines to make corrections at the main base to save expensive maintenance away from home. There were also better prospects for developments based on higher engine powers. The final decision in favour of three engines was the realisation that the operation of the tri-jet over the shorter routes was no more expensive than the twin-jet.

Through the turn of the year from 1967 to 1968, both Lockheed and McDonnell Douglas were busy refining their designs to be ready for the massive anticipated orders from the major US airlines. The Lockheed submission was redefined as the L-1011-385 with a fuselage length increased to 175ft, to allow the carriage of 250 passengers from the 7,000ft runway at New York's La Guardia to Chicago. With power from three 37,000lb thrust engines, it met American Airlines' needs, but was not entirely satisfactory when studied against the transcontinental requirements of TWA and Eastern Air Lines. With the choice of the DC-10 by American Airlines, Lockheed was free to concentrate on the longer stage lengths of the other carriers. The new airliner was named TriStar, in keeping with company tradition of naming its aircraft after heavenly bodies.

By March 1968, the aircraft specifications had grown further to an all-up weight of 409,000lb, with a payload capability of 56,200lb, equivalent to a maximum of 345 passengers. The three 40,000lb thrust engines would give a cruising speed of Mach 0.8 at 35,000ft and a typical range of 3,305 miles. This was an altogether more cost effective proposal, especially as the competition was still wide open, as although the DC-10 had achieved the initial order, it was still not sufficient to launch the programme, intensifying the sales

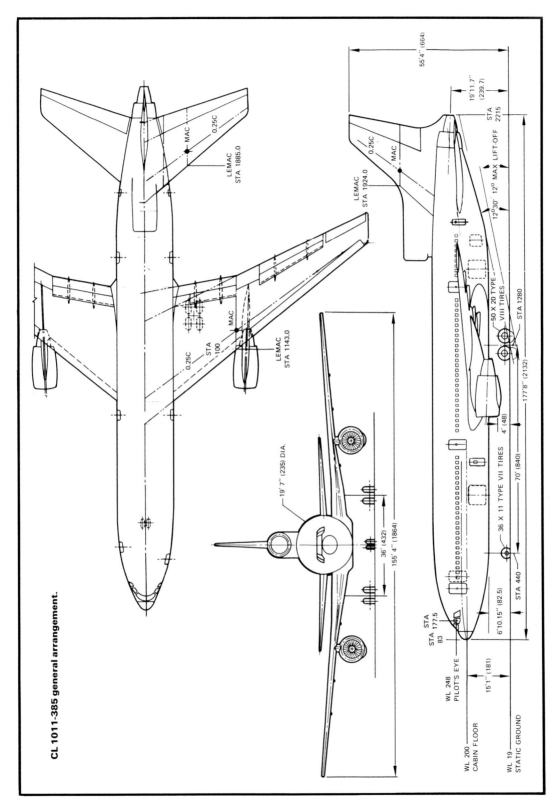

CL 1011-385 general arrangement.

LEMAC STA 1885.0
0.25C
MAC

LEMAC STA 1924.0
0.25C
MAC
55' 4'' (664)
19' 11.7'' (239.7)
STA 2215
12° MAX LIFT-OFF
12°30'
STA 1280
50 X 20 TYPE VIII TIRES
177'8'' (2132)
4' (48)
36 X 11 TYPE VII TIRES
70' (840)
STA 440
STA 177.5
STA 83
6'10.15'' (82.5)
WL 248 PILOT'S EYE
15'1'' (181)
WL 200 CABIN FLOOR
WL 19 STATIC GROUND

0.25C
STA 100
MAC
LEMAC STA 1143.0

19' 7'' (235) DIA.
36' (432)
155' 4'' (1864)

battle between Lockheed and McDonnell Douglas. To influence the imminent decision of TWA and Eastern. Lockheed offered extremely favourable terms in a buyers' market to the potential customers, a policy which was to have a major effect on subsequent events.

Both airlines were well aware of the importance of their choice to the manufacturers, and quite naturally took full advantage of the keenly competitive situation. They both decided in principle to order the Lockheed L-1011 at board meetings on 26 March 1968, but kept their decisions secret. Final discussions were held with the top management teams of McDonnell Douglas and Lockheed, beginning at the Waldorf Astoria Hotel in New York the next day. A press conference was scheduled for 11.00am on 29 March in the hotel to announce the winner, but it was not until the previous evening that TWA came to final agreement with Lockheed, and then informed McDonnell Douglas and Eastern Airlines of the decision. Eastern confirmed its plans later the same evening and Letters of Intent were signed over breakfast the next morning in time for the press announcement, launching the Lockheed L-1011 TriStar into production and development.

The definitive L-1011 which won a record value of $2,160 million orders for an airliner still on the drawing board could seat 227 passengers in a mixed-class layout or 300 all economy-class. With 227 seats, the aircraft had a US coast to coast payload-range capability with a cabin capacity load. It could also carry a maximum payload out of La Guardia on a hot day with enough fuel to reach Chicago.

The L-1011 was designed from the start with the capability to be increased in size. This was matched by the expected growth of the Rolls-Royce RB211 engines to a thrust of 50,000lb. Extra fuel tankage in the centre section and fin gave transatlantic range. As an alternative, a short-range, high-density version could have a fuselage stretch of up to 40ft to give an all economy-class capacity of over 400 passengers. Cut down twin-engined versions were still being considered to compete with the European Airbus on short ranges.

The design range of the initial version was set at 3,160 miles with a 56,200lb payload at an economical cruising speed of 565mph or Mach 0.85 at between 31,000ft and 35,000ft. At a gross weight of 409,000lb the L-1011 would take off to an altitude of 35ft in a distance of 8,750ft at sea level in standard ISA conditions.

With Boeing, McDonnell Douglas and Lockheed all developing large new commercial aircraft, there was a rush to obtain commitments from suppliers and subcontractors in order to achieve the necessary priority and quality. Lockheed made enquiries from European manufacturers as well as American ones, the first major subcontract being for the wing construction by Avco Aerostructures in Nashville, Tennessee. Main construction of the L-1011 was planned at Burbank, California, with final assembly and testing at Palmdale.

When Lockheed made the decision to go ahead with the TriStar programme in mid-1968, construction began of a whole new purpose-designed manufacturing facility at Palmdale. The area encouraged aerospace expansion and the good, year-round weather record would cut down flight testing delays. The Lockheed-California company purchased 677 acres of land and built its 'Star Factory in the Desert', designated Plant 10. Costing more than $50 million, the seven-building complex was designed specifically to incorporate the most advanced concepts in aircraft production and logistical support. The vast main assembly building has a floor space of nearly 1.3 million sq ft under one roof and more than 6,000 people were employed there during peak production. Had the demand required it, a production rate of up to 10 TriStars per month could have been achieved. The transformation of the desert site into a modern manufacturing unit took two years of massive civil engineering effort.

TriStar subassemblies and production materials were delivered by road, air and rail, the latter being along a specially built spur into a wing of the main assembly building. The main floor was split into two areas, one side for TriStar fuselage assembly, and the other side a double track final assembly area.

Much of the TriStar came from risk-sharing subcontractors and specialist suppliers, the most important of which being Rolls-Royce which supplied the RB211 engines. This subject is dealt with on its own in a later chapter.

The TriStar wings were produced by Avco Aerostructures in a contract worth $575 million. Each wing was 88ft long, 24ft wide at the root and tapering to 4ft wide at the tip. Avco had already produced the wings for the C-130 Hercules since 1954, followed by the C-141, and then the massive wing structures for the C-5 military transport. The TriStar wing contract covered an initial build of 350 sets of wings, but unfortunately only 250 aircraft were eventually produced.

The passenger and cargo doors were manufactured by Kawasaki in Japan; from Canada, Northwest Industries produced pressure bulkhead and floor structures and Bristol Aerospace built the aft engine duct. In the USA, Aeronca built the wingflaps and Murdock Engineering produced the engine support pylons. The main and nose landing gear was designed and supplied by

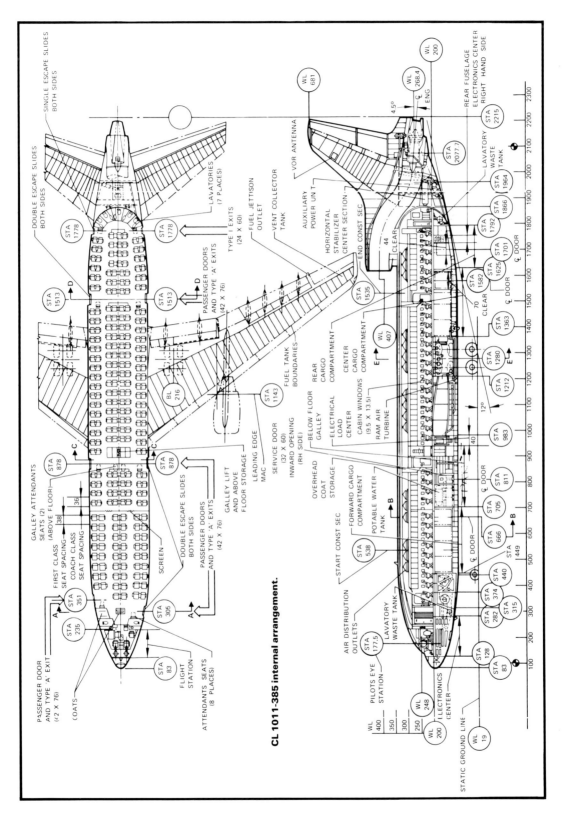

CL 1011-385 internal arrangement.

11

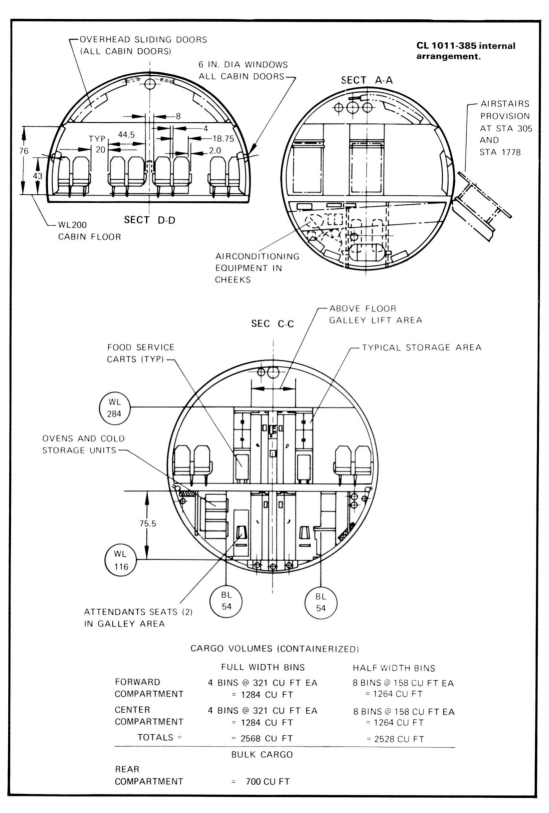

OVERHEAD SLIDING DOORS
(ALL CABIN DOORS)

6 IN. DIA WINDOWS
ALL CABIN DOORS

CL 1011-385 internal arrangement.

SECT A-A

AIRSTAIRS
PROVISION
AT STA 305
AND
STA 1778

SECT D-D

WL200
CABIN FLOOR

AIRCONDITIONING
EQUIPMENT IN
CHEEKS

SEC C-C

ABOVE FLOOR
GALLEY LIFT AREA

FOOD SERVICE
CARTS (TYP)

TYPICAL STORAGE AREA

WL
284

OVENS AND COLD
STORAGE UNITS

WL
116

ATTENDANTS SEATS (2)
IN GALLEY AREA

BL
54

BL
54

CARGO VOLUMES (CONTAINERIZED)

	FULL WIDTH BINS	HALF WIDTH BINS
FORWARD COMPARTMENT	4 BINS @ 321 CU FT EA = 1284 CU FT	8 BINS @ 158 CU FT EA = 1264 CU FT
CENTER COMPARTMENT	4 BINS @ 321 CU FT EA = 1284 CU FT	8 BINS @ 158 CU FT EA = 1264 CU FT
TOTALS =	= 2568 CU FT	= 2528 CU FT

BULK CARGO

REAR COMPARTMENT	= 700 CU FT

Menasco in Texas, while Goodrich supplied the wheels, tyres and brakes, and Goodyear the anti-skid system. Lear Siegler supplied the flight control system, Sperry produced the air data computer and Collins the avionic flight control system. Many other companies in the USA were suppliers of the remainder of the specialised systems and equipment with Lockheed producing the major portions of the airframe apart from the wings. The first wing from Avco was flown by Super Guppy from Nashville to Palmdale on 27 April 1970, followed a few days later by the other wing. These wings were produced by Avco from a new purpose-built facility with an area of 50,000sq ft. By the end of 1971, 17 complete sets of wings had been shipped to Palmdale, but by then it had been decided to transport them by rail.

Lockheed designed and built most of its production tooling itself, often having to overcome greater problems than with the construction of the aircraft. The major tooling was produced by the experienced craftsmen at Burbank, a typical task being the huge jig for the

assembly of fuselage panels. New fabrication techniques had to be developed, the side walls of the main passenger cabin being an example. The semi-monocoque shell was constructed with tapered frames and thick skins reducing the need for stringers along the inside of the skin. The double curvature sections were initially formed over large stretcher presses, and strengthening panels were bonded to improve fatigue life, corrosion resistance and durability. Some of the panels were up to 15ft wide by 38ft long and

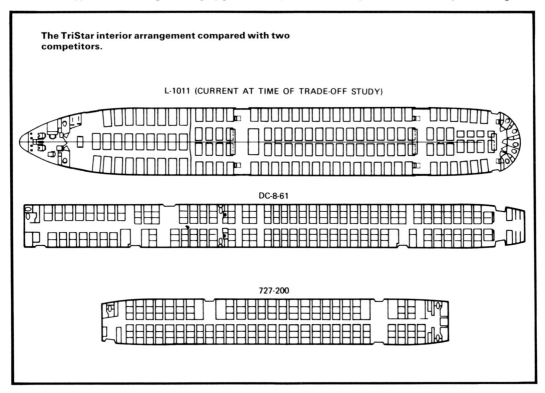

The TriStar interior arrangement compared with two competitors.

L-1011 (CURRENT AT TIME OF TRADE-OFF STUDY)

DC-8-61

727-200

Above:
The cabin was constructed with tapered frames and thick skins with no stringers along the inside of the fuselage. The centre section had the wing support structure below the floor.

Left:
The massive pressure bulkhead at the rear of the cabin is only exposed during construction and major maintenance.

required the largest autoclave in the aerospace industry to pressure cook the panels. This allowed the adhesive to cure and bond the metal, avoiding drilling holes and weakening the structure by the traditional rivet method of fastening.

The third largest building in the Lockheed complex at Palmdale was the specially developed paint hangar where the complete fuselage was painted before moving into the final assembly area. The aim was to produce a better standard of paint finish and a more efficient method of application. Using a special mobile gantry, a coat of paint could be applied in 40min to the 178ft-long fuselage, the total job requiring 58gal of polyurethane paint. The painted fuselage was then mated with the unpainted wings, to allow final assembly, roll out and predelivery flight test. The aircraft then re-entered the paint hangar for

spraying of the wings and any touching up if required elsewhere. Horizontal and vertical stabilisers were painted separately prior to mating in the main assembly building. The purpose-built plant could handle a total of 39 TriStars in the assembly jigs, on the production line and on the flight line. At full production rate, it would have had the capacity to deliver an aircraft every two days.

Fabrication of the first TriStar commenced on 1 March 1969, with assembly starting on 24 June. The assembly of the first fuselage was completed in April 1970, starting with the cockpit and forward fuselage section being mated with the mid-fuselage in a massive custom-built docking jig. This was followed soon after by the rear cabin up to and including the pressure dome. Following the delivery of the first set of wings, they were mated to the fuselage five days later. In June the

Right:
After the wings were attached the TriStars moved down the final assembly line where equipping was completed.

Rolls-Royce RB211 engines arrived and, following a rigid test programme, were installed in the aircraft ready for the official roll-out on 1 September 1970. The new factory was being constructed as the first TriStar moved through its assembly stages. When the new building was dedicated by Ronald Reagan, then Governor of the State of California, on 20 July 1970, the first TriStar was structurally complete.

During construction of the first TriStar and the build up of production, a number of important tests had been undertaken. In early 1970, the main landing gear started a rigorous 10-week programme of drop-tower testing, slamming it into the ground at various simulated landing weights, forward speeds and sink rates. The main wheels were spun up to simulate forward motion.

By July 1970, fabrication of the fatigue test specimen fuselage has commenced, with assembly started on the fifth flight test fuselage. The fatigue test specimen was rolled off the production line in December 1970, ready to commence a two-year programme to simulate 36,000 flights. These tests were undertaken in a

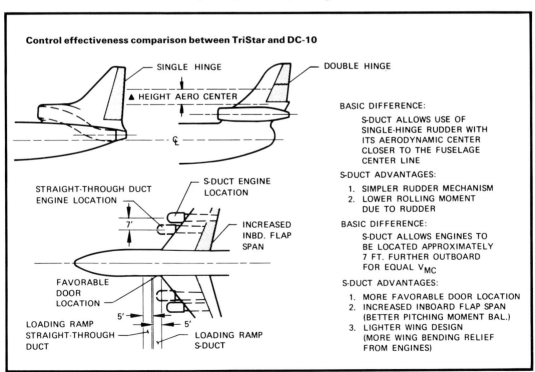

Control effectiveness comparison between TriStar and DC-10

SINGLE HINGE — DOUBLE HINGE

▲ HEIGHT AERO CENTER

STRAIGHT-THROUGH DUCT ENGINE LOCATION

S-DUCT ENGINE LOCATION

7'

INCREASED INBD. FLAP SPAN

FAVORABLE DOOR LOCATION

LOADING RAMP STRAIGHT-THROUGH DUCT

5'

5'

LOADING RAMP S-DUCT

BASIC DIFFERENCE:
S-DUCT ALLOWS USE OF SINGLE-HINGE RUDDER WITH ITS AERODYNAMIC CENTER CLOSER TO THE FUSELAGE CENTER LINE

S-DUCT ADVANTAGES:
1. SIMPLER RUDDER MECHANISM
2. LOWER ROLLING MOMENT DUE TO RUDDER

BASIC DIFFERENCE:
S-DUCT ALLOWS ENGINES TO BE LOCATED APPROXIMATELY 7 FT. FURTHER OUTBOARD FOR EQUAL V_{MC}

S-DUCT ADVANTAGES:
1. MORE FAVORABLE DOOR LOCATION
2. INCREASED INBOARD FLAP SPAN (BETTER PITCHING MOMENT BAL.)
3. LIGHTER WING DESIGN (MORE WING BENDING RELIEF FROM ENGINES)

special building which also housed the static test specimen as part of the overall structural testing activity.

Following the official roll-out, the first TriStar was moved into the adjacent Flight Test Hangar to be prepared for its maiden flight, including engine runs, installation and calibration of flight test instrumentation and taxi trials. On 16 November 1970, the aircraft lifted off for its maiden flight with L-1011 Project Pilot Hank Dees in command. The take-off weight was 330,000lb including 85,000lb of fuel and 40,000lb of test equipment. Lift-off was at 152kt after a take-off run of 5,300ft and during the 2½hr flight an altitude of 20,000ft and a speed of 250kt were reached. The engines were impressively quiet and handling characteristics were better than predicted by the engineering simulator. This was the start of a 1,500-flight test programme, totalling almost 1,700 flying hours on six aircraft.

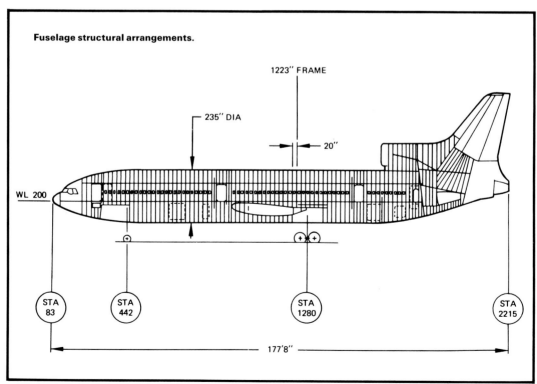

Fuselage structural arrangements.

1223" FRAME

235" DIA

20"

WL 200

STA 83

STA 442

STA 1280

STA 2215

177'8"

TriStar structure.

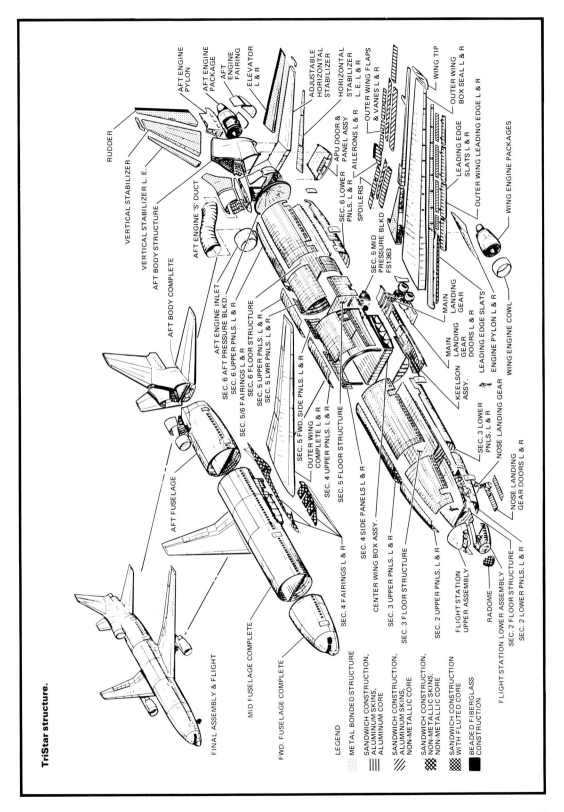

RUDDER

AFT ENGINE PYLON

AFT ENGINE PACKAGE

AFT ENGINE FAIRING

ELEVATOR L & R

ADJUSTABLE HORIZONTAL STABILIZER

HORIZONTAL STABILIZER L.E. L & R

OUTER WING FLAPS & VANES L & R

WING TIP

OUTER WING BOX SEAL L & R

OUTER WING LEADING EDGE L & R

VERTICAL STABILIZER

VERTICAL STABILIZER L. E.

AFT BODY STRUCTURE

AFT ENGINE 'S' DUCT

AFT BODY COMPLETE

AFT ENGINE INLET

SEC. 6 AFT PRESSURE BLKD.

SEC. 6 UPPER PNLS. L & R

SEC. 5/6 FAIRINGS L & R

SEC. 6 FLOOR STRUCTURE

SEC. 5 UPPER PNLS. L & R

SEC. 5 LWR PNLS. L & R

APU DOOR & PANEL ASSY

AILERONS L & R

SPOILERS

SEC. 6 LOWER PNLS. L & R

SEC. 5 MID PRESSURE BLKD FS1363

LEADING EDGE SLATS L & R

OUTER WING LEADING EDGE L & R

WING ENGINE PACKAGES

SEC. 5 FWD. SIDE PNLS. L & R

OUTER WING COMPLETE L & R

SEC. 4 UPPER PNLS. L & R

SEC. 5 FLOOR STRUCTURE

MAIN LANDING GEAR

MAIN LANDING GEAR DOORS L & R

KEELSON ASSY.

LEADING EDGE SLATS

ENGINE PYLON L & R

WING ENGINE COWL

AFT FUSELAGE

SEC. 4 FAIRINGS L & R

SEC. 4 SIDE PANELS L & R

CENTER WING BOX ASSY.

SEC. 3 UPPER PNLS. L & R

SEC. 3 FLOOR STRUCTURE

SEC. 2 UPPER PNLS. L & R

FLIGHT STATION UPPER ASSEMBLY

SEC. 3 LOWER PNLS. L & R

NOSE LANDING GEAR

NOSE LANDING GEAR DOORS L & R

FINAL ASSEMBLY & FLIGHT

MID FUSELAGE COMPLETE

FWD. FUSELAGE COMPLETE

RADOME

FLIGHT STATION LOWER ASSEMBLY

SEC. 2 FLOOR STRUCTURE

SEC. 2 LOWER PNLS. L & R

LEGEND

METAL BONDED STRUCTURE

SANDWICH CONSTRUCTION, ALUMINUM SKINS, ALUMINUM CORE

SANDWICH CONSTRUCTION, ALUMINUM SKINS, NON-METALLIC CORE

SANDWICH CONSTRUCTION, NON-METALLIC SKINS, NON-METALLIC CORE

SANDWICH CONSTRUCTION WITH FLUTED CORE

BEADED FIBERGLASS CONSTRUCTION

2 Financial Burdens

The TriStar programme became notorious for the financial problems which caused not only the near collapse of Lockheed, but the bankruptcy of Rolls-Royce. Both the airframe and engine were launched at a time of high inflation and a corresponding reduction in demand for airline seats, which made both of the major parts of the programme too expensive to finance out of existing sales. The highly competitive market helped the buyers, but caused the manufacturers to underprice their products to uneconomic levels to gain a hopefully long-term foothold in the market. The gamble eventually paid off for Rolls-Royce, but was not a complete success for Lockheed.

Lockheed's profit of £18.5 million in 1968 was followed by a loss of £13.58 million in 1969, the TriStar being a major factor in this negative figure due to the growing costs of development. This would not normally be a major problem if the other programmes were profitable, but they were not.

On 2 March 1970, the Chairman of Lockheed Aircraft, then the largest US defence contractor, requested £267 million as advanced payments to save the company from financial crisis. The programmes causing concern were the C-5A Galaxy heavy lift transport aircraft which was being produced under a fixed price contract and was subject to cost overruns of around £834 million ($2,000 million); the Cheyenne helicopter which had been cancelled by the US Army, costing Lockheed up to $110 million; the short-range attack missile (SRAM) and naval contracts. Amongst the reasons for the Galaxy cost overruns were a reduction in the size of the order and structural problems with the wing of this massive aircraft.

The US Government had a number of choices, including revising the contracts in Lockheed's

Below:
When flight testing of the RB211 commenced in the specially converted VC-10 G-AXLR, major problems were found with the performance of the engine. The soaring development costs of the RB211 engine caused the financial collapse of Rolls-Royce.
Rolls-Royce

favour in the interest of national defence, or less attractive alternatives, such as reorganisation of the company, a merger or bankruptcy proceedings. Lockheed maintained that only the four disputed programmes were in need of finance, all other projects being unaffected, with some $5,000 million worth of forward orders, and adequate credit from the banks. The urgent need was for an improvement in the short-term cash flow.

The first public signs of escalating costs with the RB211 engine were revealed by Rolls-Royce in May 1970 when the Government-sponsored Industrial Reorganisation Corporation (IRC), loaned the company £20 million to help finance the engine development for the Lockheed TriStar, the sole customer for the RB211-22. Inflation had increased overall development costs more than anticipated, but costs had also been increased by the technical difficulties with the application of carbon-fibre materials. In order to join the competitive big fan engine business against such well established US corporations as General Electric and Pratt & Whitney, Rolls-Royce had needed to reduce the price of its product to an unacceptable and uneconomic level. The IRC loan was to provide the cash flow until a positive income could be made on production deliveries, £10 million being available immediately.

To give some idea of the scale of the financial problems concerned, the Rolls-Royce Dart engine sold for £7,000 each in 1953 with sales continuing into the 1980s at prices reflecting inflation; the original selling price of the Spey engine was £65,000 and in 1970 the RB211 for the TriStar was expected to sell for initially over £250,000. There was, therefore, no way that the RB211 engine could be financed out of existing sales, especially as the company was also developing other engines. However, in order to stay in the civil aero engine business, it was imperative to bring out new products to match those of the competitors. The problems caused with the weight-saving carbon-fibre fan blades required more time than originally anticipated, resulting in the substitution of heavier titanium blades at an increased cost due to the additional engineering. The British Government had originally agreed to finance 70% of the RB211 development costs, but these were based on a fixed price estimate and did not take account of cost increases in development or escalating costs due to inflation. Any additional RB211 developments for other applications remained shelved due to lack of finance.

Lockheed announced a half-year profit of $8.3 million in August 1970, which was better than expected. However, the C-5A problem remained unresolved with a possibility that production would cease after 31 aircraft were completed, leaving a further 50 in various stages of construction out of the total order for 115 aircraft. This would result in a $1,000 million loss to the US Government, where a $200 million aid payment would provide cash flow until TriStar deliveries commenced at the end of 1971.

On the occasion of the first TriStar roll-out on 1 September 1970, orders for the aircraft were hovering at about 80% of the reported break-even figure of 225 aircraft, but some of these claimed orders were termed as second buys or options on which deposits had been paid. To take full advantage of the market, Lockheed wanted to offer a longer-range TriStar, and with the non availability of more powerful developments of the RB211, was considering the General Electric (GE) CF 6-50 as used in the competing DC-10-30. The GE engine would have only given a modest increase in range for further high development costs, unaffordable by Lockheed.

To overcome some of the immediate cash flow problems, Lockheed had negotiated a financial package with the consortium of 24 banks for a £12.5 million loan, bringing total borrowings to £146 million ($350 million) with a further loan in prospect. The major launch airlines were protecting their interests by making additional advance payments.

Frederick Corfield, the British Minister of Aviation Supply announced in the House of Commons on 11 November 1970 that the cost of launching the Rolls-Royce RB211-22 had risen from the estimated £75 million to £135 million. The original expected cost of the programme was £65 million. The Government had decided to provide a further £42 million launching aid, over the £47 million originally agreed. On the same day Rolls-Royce announced losses of £48.1 million in the first 24 weeks of the year, mainly related to the RB211 programme. As a result, Lord Cole was appointed Chairman in the place of Sir Denning Pearson.

Apart from technical difficulties with the engines, including the carbon-fibre fan blades and combustion chambers, the major financial problems were losses against contracted prices. The fixed price contract (worth £180 million when it was announced) covered 600 engines over a five-year period. Although an escalation clause was included it was inadequate to avoid a substantial loss on the contract.

To help recover some of the costs, Lockheed increased the price of the TriStar by 4% in January 1971, to be effective on orders after 1 February. The price increase of £250,000 on the original £6.25 million ($15 million) basic price included rises in the RB211 selling price. It was also felt by the US Government that Lockheed should accept a loss of about £83 million ($200 million) on the C-5A and Cheyenne programmes.

Then on 4 February 1971 came the financial collapse of Rolls-Royce, when the company announced that it was not possible to proceed with the RB211 under the present contract with Lockheed. The estimate of the launching costs had grown to £170 million and the cost of producing each of the first 540 engines would be £110,000 more than the contract price of £350,000. The possibility of an unquantifiable claim for damages from Lockheed was the main factor in the decision to put Rolls-Royce into receivership. The remainder of the aero engine business was profitable, but much of the promised additional funding had not been forthcoming, as it was conditional upon satisfactory reports by accountants. Rising costs, technical problems and late deliveries all conspired to bring about the collapse. The loss of resources already committed to the RB211, combined with the losses arising out of termination, were likely to exceed the net tangible assets of the company. The British Government acquired the assets essential to the defence of the country, and to air forces and airlines throughout the world. The assets required to safeguard the international collaborative programmes were also acquired. The continuation of the RB211 programme was to be assessed.

Rolls-Royce in effect became a nationalised company. To allow the receiver time to negotiate a new contract for the RB211 with Lockheed, the British Government permitted necessary work to continue on the engine to keep the options open on the continuation of the programme. Meanwhile Lockheed briefed its TriStar customers in New York on 9 February, but little could come out in the way of decision, since the future of the RB211 was so ill-defined. Lockheed had hoped for the future of the engine to be settled by 26 February, but the financial assessment of the company could not be completed in such a short time. Meanwhile legislation enabling the British Government to purchase the assets of Rolls-Royce received full Parliamentary approved on 15 February, but did not give a commitment to the RB211.

The new company, known as Rolls-Royce (1971) Ltd, was registered on 23 February as a nationalised company managed by a new nine-man board of directors, headed by Lord Cole. Daniel Haughton, Chairman of Lockheed, began talks in London with the new board in early March on the future of the engine. Meanwhile the Government continued to indemnify the work in progress on the RB211.

Also in early March the British Government proposed that it should set up a joint RB211 management company with Lockheed to complete development and production of the engine. Britain would invest £60 million, if Lockheed would finance the balance. There were, however, differences of opinion on how much extra money would be required to produce engines to a contract standard acceptable to the airlines. Lord Carrington, the British Minister of Defence also required a guarantee from Lockheed on the whole of any future British contribution, should the company or the TriStar collapse.

At the same time the financial report did not make encouraging reading. Not only were the additional Research & Development (R&D) costs very high, but the engine unit price was likely to be between £150,000 and £190,000 more than the original price of £350,000. Hopes were fading, for the RB211 as a change to the JT9D or CF-6 would probably cost about $50 million and with the slipping RB211 timescale, the adaptation would not be much later. The airline customers were reluctant to cancel in favour of the DC-10 as they had already invested substantial sums of money in deposit with Lockheed. The CF-6 engine appeared to be the major competitor, General Electric being able to afford to buy into the TriStar programme. As time moved on, the RB211 engine appeared less vital and the negotiating position of the British Government became weaker. Meanwhile the delivery of the engines continued to Lockheed to sustain the flight development programme. Apart from the future business loss to Rolls-Royce, the demise of the RB211 would result in significant redundancies both with Rolls-Royce and its suppliers.

As an insurance, Delta Airlines, which was an early TriStar customer, announced an order for five McDonnell Douglas DC-10s on 18 March with options on a further three. The Delta contract with Lockheed remained, with advanced payments of $34 million (£14.2 million), which was much less than the Eastern and TWA investment. Further talks continued in Washington DC between Rolls-Royce and Lockheed at a high level, with direct access to the Government departments concerned on both sides of the Atlantic, the aim being to come to an agreement as soon as possible. Lord Carrington, the Chief British negotiator was reported to have doubled the offer of aid to Lockheed to £120 million, to finance the British contribution to the joint development, but the US Government would not guarantee British expenditure, should Lockheed become bankrupt. Another sensitive area of discussion was the increase in unit price of the engines, although the parties were still bargaining.

Finally, at the end of March, a conditional agreement was reached on a new unit price for the RB211 engines. Speculation as to the agreed price ranged from £417,000 to £490,000, but the actual figure was not to be disclosed until

Lockheed had reached some agreement with their airline customers. Negotiations commenced with Air Canada, and Eastern Airlines confirmed its approval of the increased price. The agreement obviously did not involve a joint company and was a major step in securing the future of the RB211 engine, but much had to be done, not only to gain acceptance of the Rolls-Royce situation, but also to secure the future of the financially troubled Lockheed. Despite Eastern's support for the TriStar, it also considered an alternative aircraft as an insurance.

The Lockheed negotiations included the airlines, the consortium of 24 banks financing the TriStar and US Treasury officials in order to secure an additional £63 million ($150 million) loan, on top of the £144 million ($350 million) already made available. The US Government proposed a loan guarantee to the banking consortium to cover £104 million ($250 million) in loans to support the TriStar, depending upon the approval of Congress. A further £42 million ($100 million) was expected from the airlines in down payments, which were becoming more encouraged by the increased stability of Lockheed. The production line was almost at a halt due to delivery delays with the engines, and many employees were laid off.

Details of the agreement with Lockheed and the British Government began to emerge on 10 May in a statement by Fred Corfield, Minister for Aerospace. This agreement confirmed financial support for the RB211 throughout its service life, providing the TriStar programme obtained full support. Lockheed had made concessions by waiving late delivery penalties and agreed to a £50 million price increase over the first 555 engines, giving a rise in unit cost of £46,000 per engine. There was a need to know if the airlines were still interested in the programme.

TWA stated in early May, that a condition for agreement to increase the price was that BEA place a Letter of Intent for the TriStar. However, the airline was under no Government pressure to place an order.

On 12 May, a new contract for Rolls-Royce (1971) to supply the RB211 engine for the TriStar was signed, conditional upon Congressional approval of the proposed loan guarantees by the US Government. There had in fact been a new

Below:
The continuation of the TriStar programme depended upon a US Government loan guarantee for $250 million, in addition to the loans provided by the banks and initial customers.

engine competition, but the RB211 had won on performance during flight testing, delivery schedules and costs. The engine was also to have a thrust of 42,000lb compared with the original 40,600lb without increasing fuel consumption. The British Government continued interim funding of the engine at a rate of £2 million per week pending the US Government approval.

The Lockheed financing plan required to continue the TriStar programme covered a total of $750 million broken down into a number of packages. Some $400 million had already been loaned to Lockheed by the banks, $250 million to be loaned and guaranteed by the US Government and $100 million from additional advanced payments from the customer airlines. Any further delay of around six months caused by a change of engine would require a further $100 million finance. At the end of May, Lockheed announced a $86.3 million (£35.9 million) loss for 1970, more than two and a half times the 1969 loss, largely due to the increasing commitment with the TriStar.

Delays with Congressional approval were likely to take the decision to provide financial support for Lockheed beyond the deadline set by the British Government of 8 August for support of the RB211. The British Government had, however, dropped its condition that there should be a guarantee of compensation for money spent on the engine development should the TriStar programme collapse. This condition was totally unacceptable to the US Government. Meanwhile, Lockheed was recalling some of its laid-off workers to prevent further delivery delays and the Pentagon announced on 8 June that agreement had been reached with Lockheed on the C-5A for the company to accept a $200 million loss, and the USAF to cover the remaining costs of continued production of the aircraft.

TWA also threatened to cut its losses if no agreement was reached by 8 August, the deadline set in the latest Rolls-Royce/Lockheed contract, and order DC-10s. However, 8 August was not a hard and fast cut-off point for Rolls-Royce, since it would by then have committed much of the £100 million additional development funding. In an effort to gain greater support with the US Government, the tactics were changed from support for a direct rescue of Lockheed, to providing support for any troubled company to protect the economy against serious injury. In many cases, it would not cost the US Government anything, the only requirement being to guarantee the funds from the banks in case of default. The Pentagon believed that Lockheed would have to sell 350 aircraft to break even, leaving an overall loss of $359 million on the 252 projected sales. Lockheed, however,

claimed to be able to break even on between 255 and 265 sales, and the company would anyway be able to repay all government guaranteed loans. There was also a projected market by 1980 for 775 intermediate-range tri-jets of which Lockheed expected to obtain an adequate share despite direct competition from the DC-10.

The US House of Representatives approved the Refinance Bill on 30 July with the Senate vote to follow, although the deadline of 8 August was approaching rapidly, when not only the contract between Rolls-Royce and Lockheed expired, but the US Congress went into summer recess. The House of Representatives' approval covered the financial guarantee to Lockheed alone, not a wider based legislation. The Senate was expected to vote against the Lockheed-only proposal, and the debate could be delayed by the political move of filibustering by the opponents of the Bill.

The US Senate ended six months of uncertainty about the future of the TriStar when on 2 August, the vote was in favour of a $250 million guarantee to cover continued financial support of the programme. The vote was very close, and was initially a tie, but on a second vote a member who had abstained, made the vote 49 in favour, to 48 against. Once again the vote had been to support Lockheed only, not any wider industrial difficulties. This allowed the additional $250 million to be loaned by the bank consortium, which in the event of a Lockheed bankruptcy would be paid by the US Government. The US Treasury would have first claim on the corporation's assets, and Lockheed pointed out that if the TriStar programme were to fail, the tax loss to the US Government would be in excess of the $250 million guarantee. Neither the original $400 million bank loan, nor the $100 million advance by the airlines was covered by the guarantee. Lockheed's financial difficulties were caused by losses of some $500 million on its unsuccessful military contracts, made worse by the Rolls-Royce collapse.

The RB211 engine was therefore to proceed subject to the successful ratification of the Rolls-Royce/Lockheed contract and the British Government extended the financial support of the engine until 24 August, giving 16 days in which to finalise the arrangements. The go ahead was also conditional on the airlines confirming their intentions to buy the aircraft, Delta and Air Canada being the major customers still to decide.

Despite the approval by the US government, further formalities had to be undertaken before the loan was approved. A three-man committee was set up on 25 August to approve the US Government's guarantee of finance to Lockheed. This committee, chaired by John Connally, Secretary of the US Treasury, was responsible for

receiving the formal application from Lockheed for the $250 million guarantee. Approval had to be given by this committee before Lockheed could sign up with its bankers, and the contract with Rolls-Royce could come into force. In addition the US Government had imposed a surcharge of 10% on all imports, which, despite calls for exemption, included the RB211 engines. Although this was expected to increase the cost of the total 178 TriStars on order by $55 million, the surcharge was not expected to remain for very long and could be removed before delivery of engines to the airlines. The surcharge also affected the DC-10, about 15% of which was imported.

The loan guarantee was valid until 31 December 1973, by which time enough cash was expected to be generated to pay off the debt.

On 9 September, the formal US Government approval was given to the loan guarantee and joint simultaneous contracts were signed in New York between the US Government, the banks, the airlines, Rolls-Royce and Lockheed. Final settlement was reached on 14 September 1971, allowing the TriStar programme to restart at top speed. From the all-time low of 2,640 in May the workforce at Lockheed had grown to 4,400 with 100 people per week being hired.

The final legal hurdle had been cleared for a complicated financial package involving two governments, two major companies and a group of top international airlines. Lockheed avoided bankruptcy, by a tight margin, which would have

Above:
The slowing down of the TriStar production line increased costs dramatically. Amongst the last dozen L-1011-500s to leave the line at Palmdale were those for TAP Air Portugal. *Lockheed*

been the end of the TriStar, the RB211 and many thousands of jobs with the prime contractors and their suppliers. The US Government would have lost a major defence contractor and a great deal of money in the process. It was marginal if the TriStar would make a profit on sales, but the project would be financed by other programmes, and money would be made in product support over the life of the aircraft in commercial service.

Rolls-Royce, however, survived bankruptcy with the support of the British Government, largely due to the reliance on the engines in the defence programmes in Britain and the commercial markets throughout the world. Such a company could not be sacrificed. In the event the RB211 engine went on to power the TriStar, and was successfully developed to power a number of major transport aircraft produced by Boeing. It became a cost-effective alternative in the Boeing 747 and 767 and, in a cropped version, also shares the power of the 757 with Pratt & Whitney. The continuation of the RB211 kept Rolls-Royce in the forefront of aero engine technology, and able to compete in the world market with a range of new engines. The company has now returned to private ownership.

3 Engine Development

Any one of the big three engine companies, General Electric, Pratt & Whitney or Rolls-Royce, was capable of producing a suitable engine for the TriStar. However, in 1967, when the choice had to be made, the Pratt & Whitney JT-9 engines were optimised for the thrust, diameter and nacelle configuration requirements for the Boeing 747 programme. With the tooling already being prepared, Pratt & Whitney was reluctant to make the changes required by Lockheed, including a lower thrust, better positioned acccessories and a quieter engine operation for the smaller city airports to be served by the TriStar. The level of noise being aimed for was 100db, about the same as the prop-jet Electra which had not caused too many noise complaints. Any greater noise reduction would increase costs and weight unacceptably.

General Electric was developing its TF39 engine, which could provide 41,000lb of thrust, for the giant Lockheed C-5A military transport, and offered to adapt this engine to the TriStar programme, by reducing the fan diameter, the bypass ratio and the thrust. This engine became the civil CF-6 and was eventually adopted as the DC-10 powerplant, as well as other applications.

At this time Rolls-Royce did not have a suitable engine, but had produced a prototype smaller-scale engine to demonstrate its new three-shaft technology. This new layout appeared to be a major breakthrough, but with no immediate application for this engine, Rolls-Royce was keen to scale up the engine to meet the Lockheed requirement, at the same time joining in the big league competition for future business. The accessories were arranged as required and the acoustics were tailor-made, resulting in the Rolls-Royce RB211 three-shaft, turbo-fan, high bypass engine.

This engine was chosen by Lockheed and the airlines when on 29 March 1968, it was announced that Rolls-Royce had won the biggest single export order every achieved by any section of British industry. The announcement came from a pair of hastily-convened simultaneous press conferences by Lockheed in New York and Rolls-Royce in London.

In addition to the launch orders by Eastern Airlines and TWA, an order was placed by Air Holdings of London for 30 aircraft with options on a further 20 for sale to airlines outside the USA to assist in the US balance of payments and trade due to the adoption of a British engine, instead of one from America. The value to Rolls-Royce for the initial 124 aircraft, plus 10 options equalled about £150 million, with further significant growth expected. Many major airlines, particularly in the USA, were ready to order the new generation wide-bodied jet airliners, but the DC-10 provided keen competition with its GE engines.

Development was expected at that time to cost around £50 million, and without the new programme, Rolls-Royce would be running out of work within three years, except for on the smaller engines which would be insufficient to sustain the company. There were also plans to produce the larger RB207 engine for the European Airbus, but the GE CF-6 was eventually selected as the prime power plant. Efforts to install the RB211 in the DC-10 were to no avail.

The contract for the RB211 covered the complete power plant pack, including air intake, thrust reverser, silencer nozzle, pod and pylon. The airframe parts such as the intake, pod and pylon were subcontracted to Shorts, the normal practice with Rolls-Royce.

Lockheed chose the RB211 engine for a number of reasons. The technological advantages were expected to revolutionise the commercial engine business; cost advantages in the USA and particularly elsewhere, allowing the price to be quoted in pounds sterling; and the fact the Rolls-Royce expertise would allow the engine to be tailor-made to Lockheed's requirements. The need was for a 40,000lb thrust engine, improved fuel consumption over existing engines, a low specific weight, low noise level to the community and passengers, reduced smoke emission, simplicity of construction and maintenance.

As far back as 1964, Rolls-Royce had started an advanced technology exercise around a two-shaft turbo-fan RB178 engine developing 27,000lb thrust. This engine technology was to match the increasing size of the projected transport aircraft, although the wide-bodied types were still to be seriously considered. As the bigger airliners were studied, the major limitation appeared to be the available power sources, and the RB178 grew in size to a projected thrust of 44,000lb. This engine was aimed at the Boeing 747 requirement following in 1966 with a series of detail design studies for a new generation of engines for subsonic transport. From these studies came a series of high bypass, three-shaft engine projects ranging from 10,000lb to 50,000lb thrust.

Above:
**The RB211 VC10 engine testbed G-AXLR was fitted
with an alternator loading pod under the starboard
wing to boost the total electrical load, to simulate
that of the TriStar.** *P. J. Birtles*

The RB211, detail design of which commenced in July 1967, featured a bypass ratio of 5 : 1 which in effect meant that a large front fan acting like a multiblade propeller produced over 70% of the engine's thrust from the air which bypassed the turbojet core. Normally this system was operated using two concentric shafts, one to drive the fan, but the three-shaft layout introduced a third stage, one driving the fan and the other two driving their individual turbines. This resulted in 25% fewer parts needed to generate the required thrust, achievement of the high pressure ratio and high bypass ratio with a 25% improvement in fuel consumption over the two-shaft engines, and a reduction in engine speed which significantly reduces the noise, due to the slower-moving greater volume of air.

To meet the simplified maintenance requirement, the engine was designed around seven basic independent modules. This allowed rapid change of each module without removing the engine, and the determination of a service life for each module rather than the worst case covering the entire engine. Major economic improvements were made on engine overhaul costs and spares holdings.

The initial order placed by Lockheed with Rolls-Royce was for 555 engines and spares worth more than $450 million. The original RB211-22 engine was expected to have a take-off thrust of between 37,020lb and 40,600lb at sea level, with a planned thrust growth to 50,000lb without any increase in diameter. This increase in thrust would be achieved by redistributing more air through the gas generator section from the bypass. The advantages of the three spools, as against the competing two-spool engines, would result in a smaller engine for a given pressure ratio, because the compressors and turbines were running under near-optimum conditions. Simplicity was helped by having no moving stators, lower approach noise levels because of front fan speed control, and a greater thrust-growth potential.

One of the most significant areas of engineering experience to be used in the RB211 was the lightweight Hyfil fan blade of composite carbon-fibre construction and smaller diameter glass composite low pressure compressor blades. The Hyfil fan blades were developed through Rolls-Royce's work on lightweight lift engines and gave lightness, low cost and stiffness and allowed the deletion of noise generating mid-span shrouds. Rolls-Royce could also claim major advances in turbine blade cooling in civil operations with experience of around 14 million hr, and individual blade lives achieving 16,000hr. Only modest advances in blade cooling techniques were anticipated with the higher temperature to be used.

Construction of the 13 development engines commenced at Derby, with the first one making its initial run on the test stand on 31 August 1968. The development programme consisted initially of ground testing, in particular in the high-altitude test facility of the British National Gas Turbine Establishment (NGTE) at Pyestock, where it was possible to simulate most of the L-1011 flight envelope. The noise tests at the Rolls-Royce Flight Test Establishment at Hucknall near Derby included an engine mounted in its underwing nacelle and also in a mock-up of the aft fuselage 'S' duct intake arrangement. Complete engine mock-ups were shipped to Lockheed to study the installation and maintenance problems. Initial testing of the reverse-thrust system was undertaken on the 11th engine in the development programme, using several new and unique features. Fan stream was reversed by moving rearwards an annular section of the fan cowling to uncover the deflecting cascade vanes, and at the same time closing reverser flaps over the fan duct outlet. Simultaneously a target type spoiler was deployed to neutralise the thrust of the gas generator exhaust.

Clearing of the RB211 for flight testing commenced in early January 1970, ready for installation in a VC10 transport loaned to Rolls-Royce from the RAF. The RB211 test engine was installed in place of the port pair of Rolls-Royce Conway engines. This modified VC10 made its maiden flight from Hucknall on 6 March

1970 lasting 80min, followed later the same day by another flight of 56min. The engine performance was completely satisfactory within the flight regime explored of up to 15,000ft altitude and a speed of 400kt. The test installation was representative of the TriStar, using the same attachment points and the VC10 was able to accurately perform to the majority of the TriStar limits. This initial flight test was the start of a planned 1,100hr flight development programme.

The test RB211 was mounted so as to reproduce the correct intake conditions during cruising flight of the wing-mounted units on the TriStar. Adjustments had to be made to install the engine in the VC10, in particular the hot stream spoiler of the thrust reverser was rotated through 48° to avoid re-ingestion problems resulting from the rear fuselage position. The VC10 systems were modified to suit the engine, using where possible TriStar instrumentation. Wheel brake cooling fans were added to adapt the normally long-haul VC10 to the intensive short/medium-haul TriStar type of operation with rapid turnrounds.

The flight tests were able to explore the full altitude and Mach-number envelope of the engine; to make noise, cooling and vibration tests; to establish engine management techniques and the required flightdeck instrumentation. In addition to being able to study maintenance and accessibility, the VC10 installation helped establish initial service life and the assessment of spares requirements.

Out of a total of 19 experimental engines for the bench development programme, 18 were running by the time of the first test flight, and from the eighth engine which first ran on 31 July 1969 all had been built to TriStar flight installation standards. The prototype engines for the first TriStar were under construction.

The development work included aerodynamic, performance and strain-gauge testing to determine stress levels, noise and smoke evaluation and simulated flight cycle endurance running. The full scale testing was complemented by a comprehensive rig and structural test programme, involving the assessment of some 200 different configurations of major components in 4,000hr of testing. The target rated thrust of 40,600lb was achieved by the end of 1969, but the flight testing would confirm fuel consumption figures.

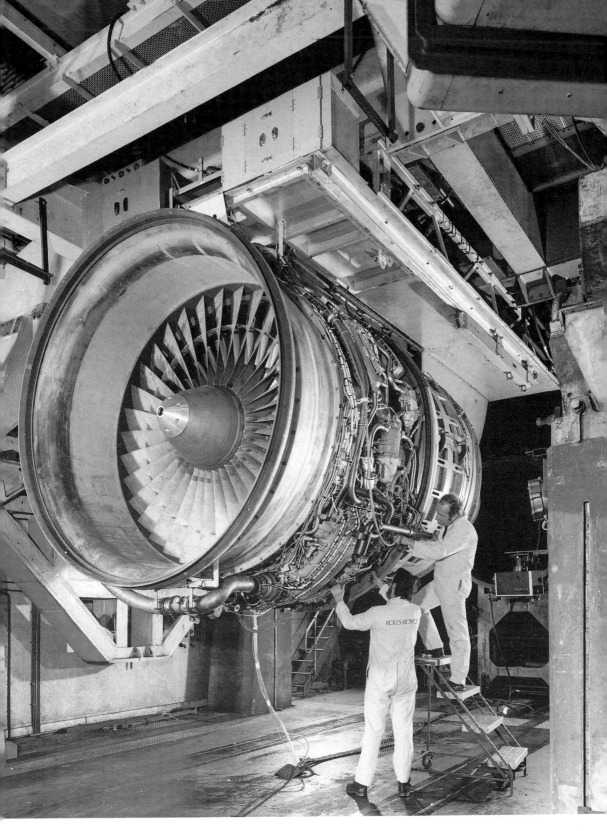

The testbeds constructed specifically by Rolls-Royce for RB211 testing were capable of accepting engines with a thrust of up to 70,000lb. Tests were conducted to confirm that the casing and carcase of the engine were distortion free, the three-shaft design helping to keep the carcase short and therefore stiff. The NGTE tests proved that the RB211 could be relit up to the maximum cruise pressure altitude of the TriStar.

Confidence in the engine was such that component manufacture was well advanced for the production standard engines, including all the main gas generator items for the first TriStar engines. A new 200,000sq ft floor area manufacturing plant was constructed at Avonmouth, near Bristol, to handle production of the Hyfil fan blades, a test programme of over 16,000hr being run using blades of the new material in Conway engines powering the BOAC VC10 fleet.

As an insurance, Rolls-Royce also used titanium for the compressor fan in case of problems with Hyfil, even though titanium was heavier and more expensive. As a result the test programme had to be duplicated to some extent which resulted in increased costs. In the event this insurance paid dividends as during initial flight testing there were bird and grit ingestion problems with the Hyfil blades. This resulted in much of the development programme being done with the titanium blades. One of the problems with Hyfil blades was found to be grit erosion causing partial delamination by water penetration during flights through tropical rainstorms. These problems had been found during the BOAC endurance testing with VC10s, and were therefore well known by Rolls-Royce, but not revealed until a month into the flight development programme.

Below:
Once the financial difficulties with Rolls-Royce had been resolved, production of the RB211-22 engines was able to commence. The RB211 engines were assembled for ease of access in the vertical position.
Rolls-Royce

The grit and rain erosion problem was overcome by plating the leading edge of the blade with nickel and treating the remainder with polyurethane paint. However, in the bird impact case, even with the addition of steel or titanium spines bonded into the leading edge, the shear strength was insufficient to avoid structural failure. An answer was to laminate with steel inserts to provide the required strength through multiple load paths, forming the basis for a solution to the bird strike problem, but the delays certainly would result in the TriStar flying with the 300lb heavier (and less economic) titanium-fanned engine.

The steel inserts also caused more than just new production problems. The fatigue resistance properties were much reduced, and improvements were made by modifying the blade resin interface with the steel root.

Flutter was encountered at about 80% low-pressure spool rpm, the traditional cure being to twist the tips of the metal blades to correct the incidence. However, as carbon composite blades could not be twisted after manufacture, the dovetail root fittings had to be machined at a different angle relative to the engine-axis datum. This cured the flutter successfully. The titanium fans were expected to be £400 more expensive than the Hyfil fans, but the development problems with the composite structures were obviously adding their own increases in terms of costs, complexity of manufacture and time delays.

Progress had been limited at one stage in the development programme by the need to avoid running the engines at high speed and high temperature. This caused failure of the high pressure turbine blades due to fatigue failures at the shroud because of unexpected stresses. This was cured by a minor design change as is typical with any complex engine development programme. The oil and fuel consumption were well on target and the engine handling was well within the acceptable limits. Noise testing with the latest standard of acoustic lining allowed the aircraft to meet the stringent noise requirements.

When the first TriStar was rolled out at Palmdale on 1 September 1970, it was fitted with RB211 engines using Hyfil fan blades, but the first set of flight-rated engines, due soon after, had titanium fan blades and Hyfil was never used. Meanwhile Lockheed was looking at long-range developments of the TriStar, but the uprated RB211-50 engine required for this model would probably have cost the British taxpayer a further £100 million. Lockheed, therefore, was investigating the possibility of alternative engines from other manufacturers. Lockheed's own financial problems in fact precluded the change of engine

due to the extra development costs on the airframe.

While the flight testing progressed on the VC10, ground testing continued at the comprehensive aerodynamic test facility at Hucknall, including cross wind testing up to a 50kt wind speed, and 30kt tailwinds. The crosswinds were generated by a Proteus turboprop mounted in a duct on a mobile rig, against both the TriStar pod and 'S'-duct intakes. Full scale intake efficiency was tested by using six Avon jet engines to provide the necessary suction.

With the first TriStar in final preparation for its maiden flight, Rolls-Royce had already delivered six engines by Hercules freighter to Palmdale. The full production standard were due for delivery by the end of 1970 to power the second TriStar in its development programme. Although the initial engines were up to the 40,600lb thrust, the RB211-22B for the start of commercial operations would be capable of 42,000lb thrust. Further developments of the basic engine for other applications could see a growth to at least 50,000lb, but costs were still escalating. With improvements to blade cooling and the combustion chamber the engine could achieve 45,000lb thrust.

Test running of the engines to an ever increasing modification standard had reached nearly 3,000hr, with production engines joining the programme mainly on endurance work. Up to six '-22' production engines were proposed for this part of the programme. Although the emphasis was on combustion development, one engine concentrated on the total package testing to check systems integration and stresses due to vibration. Fuel consumption was on target and continued to improve as refinements were made to the engine. The problems with the Hyfil blades were still not entirely overcome particularly in the bird ingestion case. Hollow titanium fan blades were also being considered, giving a comparable weight saving to Hyfil.

The three-shaft layout gave good engine handling, low vibration levels and a stiff carcase. The modular construction made on the wing module changes a practical and simple operation. On condition maintenance would be possible from service entry due to numerous boroscope inspection ports. The early flight engines for the TriStar prototype were cleared for an initial life of 50 flying hours.

The RB211 gave surge-free handling during acceleration from flight idle to 95% maximum thrust in under 5sec. Climb thrust, once set, required no further throttle movement to maintain the rated value due to an altitude schedule.

As its development programme proceeded, the

VC10 test bed had flown up to 38,000ft and Mach 0.87. Relights were made from 150kt at 500ft to 300kt up to 30,000ft. The engine never failed to relight and was completely stable during aircraft stall tests. An airborne integrated data system (AIDS) with up to 30 channels was developed to monitor and record engine performance and parameters to cut down unnecessary maintenance and down time.

The technical problems with the RB211 engine were overshadowed by the financial collapse of Rolls-Royce in February 1971, although they were major contributors to the cash flow difficulties. The TriStar flight development programme was progressing well, but doubts on the continuing availability of further engines curtailed the flight testing and drastically affected production of the airframes. The RB211 engines had performed well during the test programme, a minor problem being a high pressure turbine blade failure on the 14th flight.

With the approval of the loans to Lockheed, flight testing and production of the TriStar were able to recommence at the planned rate and the 42,000lb thrust RB211 engines were flying in the second aircraft, with a further six engines to follow on 9 September 1971. Certification of the engines was planned for February 1972 coinciding with delivery of the full production standard units.

By the end of September production of the RB211 engine was building up rapidly, with more than 85% of the parts made for the first batch of 14 power plants for service with Eastern and TWA from April 1972. All 18 engines for the flight development programme were delivered by the end of 1971, and production was fully established for engine deliveries well into 1972 as part of the overall contract for 555 engines.

In early January 1972, the RB211 engine was declared ready for commercial operations. There had been no new mechanical failures and a small performance loss in the high pressure compressor had been cured. The 150hr flight test approval programme had been achieved successfully. A compressor blade crack was easily rectified by correcting a manufacturing process, turbine temperatures were within guarantees and the engines had operated successfully in freezing fog. Deliveries of engines were a few weeks behind schedule, largely due to production being ahead of modifications, but the situation was improving and TriStar customer commitments were unaffected. A 10% increase in guaranteed fuel consumption was found to be due to errors in fuel measuring equipment.

As the provisional Air Registration Board certification of the RB211 was awarded on 24 February 1972, a Government White Paper was issued detailing total cost of the engine development to the British taxpayer of between £190 and £195 million. This was some three times the figure for the original estimate of launch costs, made in 1968, of £65.5 million. This figure was £20-25 million higher than previous estimates due to a recent devaluation of the US dollar. The original launching aid had been agreed at 70% of the launching costs, subject to a maximum of £47.1 million. With the rapid escalation in development costs identified in early 1971, the company had the choice of scrapping the RB211 programme, or delaying it substantially while the engineering problems were being solved. Both courses were extremely costly. The eventual result was receivership on 4 February, with the British Government providing financial support to essential parts of the company in terms of national defence, international collaboration and commercial operations.

Full certification of the Rolls-Royce RB211-22C engine was granted by the British Air Registration Board (ARB) and US Federal Aviation Administration (FAA) on 22 March 1972. This was after a successful 150hr test run at full operating temperature, followed by a strip and inspection, clearing the engine for passenger service at a thrust of 42,000lb with performance improvements anticipated before the end of the year. One RB211 engine was being produced every working day, with some 140 due for delivery by the end of 1972. This had been achieved with a reduction in manpower since 1969 of 9,500 people to 35,500 and a reduction in floor area by 1,000,000sq ft by closing 52 sites.

Rolls-Royce had been faced with a choice of going ahead with the RB211 engine with its attendant risks, or going out of business due to lack of future expansion. The company took the gamble and failed, but a new Rolls-Royce rose again out of the ashes, with the very product that had been intended for future growth, the RB211 engine. It has proved to be technologically a great success with sufficient adaptability to be competitive with the two major American engine manufacturers. Rolls-Royce RB211 variants are being chosen by the world's airlines to power their American-built wide-bodied jets, even from well established Pratt & Whitney and GE customers. A RB211 variant has yet to find a place in a European Airbus product, which was one of the original target aircraft for the larger, but related, RB207, before the A300 reduced in size to the A300B. Meanwhile, TriStar production has ceased, and there are little prospects in the immediate future for Lockheed to re-enter the commercial jet airliner field, and if it does, it is more likely to be in collaboration with another manufacturer.

4 Flight Testing

The maiden flight of the first TriStar N1011 on 16 November 1970, from Palmdale, Ca was the start of an intensive flight development programme, involving five aircraft over a period of 12 months and including 1,695hr flying. This maiden flight, which was under the command of Hank Dees and was exactly to a schedule laid down 2½ years previously, made a take-off run of about 5,000ft in 32sec, carrying a payload of 33,000lb of test equipment. During this initial flight, which lasted for 140min, both the aircraft and its Rolls-Royce RB211-22 engines performed well. The target date for certification was set as 15 November 1971.

Two days later the aircraft was again airborne for a 2hr 45min flight concentrating on low-speed handling, and the functioning of the undercarriage and flaps. The aircraft reached a maximum speed of 300kt and an altitude of 10,000ft.

By early December the TriStar had flown about 11hr in five flights and testing included successful shutdowns and relights of Nos 1 and 2 engines and a number of touch-and-go landings. The sixth flight on 4 December was the longest to date with a time of 4hr 15min, and flights on 10 and 11 December took total flying time in less than one month to 24hr 35min. Maximum speed achieved was 350kt and the maximum take-off weight had reached 335,000lb. Air starts had been made on all three engines with and without the assistance of the Auxiliary Power Unit (APU). Although the first flight carried a crew of four, development testing required a crew of nine or 10 including flight test observers.

A total of 12 aircraft were in various stages of construction in the final assembly building, including two structural test specimens, building up to a rate of one aircraft completed every week, one year after the maiden flight of the prototype.

In parallel with the flight test programme, the structural test specimens were proving the integrity of the airframe, the fatigue specimens commencing a two-year programme in January 1971 to simulate 36,000 flights in airline operation.

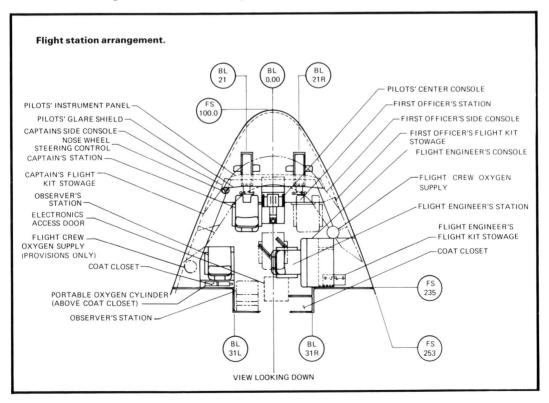

Flight station arrangement.

PILOTS' INSTRUMENT PANEL
PILOTS' GLARE SHIELD
CAPTAINS SIDE CONSOLE
NOSE WHEEL STEERING CONTROL
CAPTAIN'S STATION
CAPTAIN'S FLIGHT KIT STOWAGE
OBSERVER'S STATION
ELECTRONICS ACCESS DOOR
FLIGHT CREW OXYGEN SUPPLY (PROVISIONS ONLY)
COAT CLOSET
PORTABLE OXYGEN CYLINDER (ABOVE COAT CLOSET)
OBSERVER'S STATION

BL 21
BL 0.00
BL 21R
FS 100.0

PILOTS' CENTER CONSOLE
FIRST OFFICER'S STATION
FIRST OFFICER'S SIDE CONSOLE
FIRST OFFICER'S FLIGHT KIT STOWAGE
FLIGHT ENGINEER'S CONSOLE
FLIGHT CREW OXYGEN SUPPLY
FLIGHT ENGINEER'S STATION
FLIGHT ENGINEER'S FLIGHT KIT STOWAGE
COAT CLOSET
FS 235

BL 31L
BL 31R
FS 253

VIEW LOOKING DOWN

During the 14th flight on 23 December, the centre engine had to be shut down as a precaution when vibration occurred. During the subsequent scheduled grounding for routine systems checks and adjustments to the aircraft, it was found that a first-stage high pressure turbine blade had been damaged. The RB211, which had an early type of turbine, was stripped for examination and an improved standard of turbine module was substituted.

By the time of the financial failure of Rolls-Royce on 4 February 1971, the prototype TriStar had completed about 40hr of flight testing with the first aircraft for TWA N31001 and Eastern N301EA waiting to join the development programme.

During this early testing the prototype had achieved all its flight goals, including flying at Mach 0.7 and 300kt up to an altitude of 30,000ft. The fully forward and aft centre of gravity limits

had been explored, the approach to the stall was vice free and accelerated flight had been made up to loads of 2g. As well as aerodynamic testing, the functioning of some of the systems had been investigated, including the running of the APU which had been started at altitudes of up to 20,000ft, and had been kept running at 30,000ft. The means of generating emergency hydraulic power to supplement the engine-driven system was revised using a Dowty Rotol ram-air turbine. Although it was expected that a windmilling RB211 would provide enough emergency hydraulic power at above 200kt, at the approach speeds of below 150kt, there would be insufficient hydraulic pressure for the fully-powered flight controls, so requiring the ram-air turbine.

The RB211 engines had performed generally well although fuel consumption was between 3% and 4% above guarantees. The high pressure turbine blade failure appeared readily soluble by Rolls-Royce. The engine had been tolerant to deliberate mishandling by the test pilots with reverse thrust held in right down to zero forward speed at idle power. To minimise brake wear

during taxying, the centre engine was run in reverse, and the RB211 was shut down and started in the reverse thrust configuration, saving ground time on maintenance. There had been no effective running time limitations on the pre-production engines as when the original 25hr limit was reached, the life was extended as necessary on the basis of engine condition. Even the low speed levels of the development engines were expected to improve with the production standard. Development engines had arrived on time, but production units were between six and 12 months behind schedule.

The second TriStar, in TWA markings, joined the test programme on 15 February 1971 when it made its first flight lasting 1hr 25min from Palmdale. The new aircraft made tests on the undercarriage, flaps, slats, spoilers and the environmental control system, bringing total test flying to nearly 55hr. By early March, with TriStar No 4, originally the first for Delta, on the line, nearly 70hr flying had been completed.

Flight testing continued during the negotiations to save both Lockheed and Rolls-Royce finan-

Left:
During the flight development programme TriStar N1011 was fitted with a gust probe in the nose to measure air turbulence without interference from the airframe.

Below left:
In all commercial flight development programmes it is necessary to demonstrate the minimum unstick speed, with the rear fuselage protected by a special skid, dragging along the runway. This is to avoid stalling the aircraft during the take-off rotation.

cially, but at a somewhat reduced pace, due to uncertainties with the programme and technical problems with the engine. The prototype was grounded for a month up to 5 April for modifications and uprating of the three pre-production RB211 engines, to allow higher performance test flights to be made. On 13 April 1971, the prototype lifted its heaviest load to date, when it also flew faster and for longer than on any previous occasion. The flight was made from the long runways at Edwards Air Force Base with a take-off weight of 404,570lb. A top speed of 495kt was reached up to an altitude of 30,000ft. The aircraft was airborne for 6hr 41min, more than twice its previous longest flight. By the middle of April, the two test aircraft had logged over 90hr in the air.

On 27 April the second TriStar made its first two fully automatic landings, following one touch down with automatic control of the flying surfaces but with manual operation of the throttles. The TriStar was due to be certificated to Cat 2 standards, although it was expected to be capable of Cat 3 operations with its highly sophisticated flight control system. By the end of April, the two aircraft had made 46 flights in a flight time of 126hr.

The TriStar was expected to meet the new noise requirements called for in the new FAR 36 regulations, assisted by the use of noise-attenuated intake liners.

Although the TriStar had not flown by early May 1971 with the full 42,000lb thrust engine, the 17th delivered to Lockheed had run at 43,000lb on the test bed. Flying at that time was with the Dash 3 engines rated at 36,000lb thrust, to be followed mid-year with the Dash 3+ engines rated at 40,200lb, although both would be reduced on hot days. This increased power would be welcome in the test programme as even the early morning temperature at Palmdale was regularly 80°F. The engines had stood up well to rough handling, such as starting up with a 20kt tailwind and taxying with up to 50kt tailwinds without a problem. Only two engine in-flight

shutdowns had been made and the revised date of FAA certification of 16 April 1972 was on target. An additional 25hr would be flown on the first TriStar with ARB representatives to gain British certification soon after the achievement of FAA clearance.

On 17 May 1971, two days behind the revised schedule, the third TriStar entered the flight test programme at Palmdale. This aircraft, destined for Eastern Airlines was flown by Jack Woodman, with Hank Dees, chief test pilot for the TriStar, as co-pilot. Total flight time had reached 160hr.

The first TriStar for Eastern Airlines attended the Paris Show at Le Bourget in June 1971, its first international flight. The quietness of the engines was particularly impressive. The flight from Palmdale was made in four legs taking 12hr, bringing the total flying to around 200hr, with about 25hr on the particular aircraft. Cruise speed across the Atlantic was Mach 0.81 at a height of 33,000ft. Take-off from Goose Bay, after changing an accessory gearbox in the port engine, was at a weight of 378,000lb, landing 4hr later at Shannon. The RB211 engines were achieving at least 42,000lb thrust, while some were achieving 46,000lb with adequate growth potential. The engine noise was well below the FAR 36 noise limitations, its typical approach level being 102.5PNdB. On its return flight to the USA, the TriStar visited East Midlands Airport in Britain to be viewed by Rolls-Royce employees.

By 25 June, three TriStars had made 109 flights, 58 by the first aircraft, 28 by the second and 23 by the third. Maximum speed attained was Mach 0.91, maximum altitude 37,500ft and the highest take-off weight was 404,570lb. Maximum indicated airspeed registered below 22,000ft had been 440kt, slightly better than the design speed at that altitude. Twenty-nine automatic landings had been made and 35 pilots from actual or potential customers had flown the aircraft. Flutter testing had been practically completed, giving a clean bill of health in all flight regimes. The engines had continued to perform well, being responsive to rapid accelerations and decelerations. Twenty flight-rated engines had been delivered including eight rated at more than 40,000lb thrust.

The RB211 engines had logged 1,000hr of test flying in the TriStar by mid-July on the 127th test flight. With the engines developing 42,000lb thrust, the TriStar was able to prove its performance limits by reaching its design altitude of 42,000ft and a maximum design speed of 660mph (Mach 0.95) in a shallow dive from 40,000ft.

Noise measurements taken during the first eight months of TriStar testing showed that the three RB211 engines would be substantially quieter than the minimum levels laid down by the FAA, the regulations permitting up to 105.6PNdB for take-off at maximum weight and power. The TriStar had been achieving 97.8PNdB. On the approach the regulations are 107PNdB while the TriStar measured 102.3. These measurements are on a logarithmic scale, giving 60% to 70% less noise nuisance than the aircraft which it was to replace in airline service.

The autoland programme progressed well, with more than 40 fully automatic landings made by the end of July, and the three test aircraft had flown about 420hr.

With the political and financial problems removed in September 1971, the flight testing of TriStar continued in the near ideal weather conditions at Palmdale. More than 540hr had been flown, exploring the flight envelope in some cases beyond the required limits. High-Mach behaviour had been investigated to Mach 0.958 providing an ample margin of flutter clearance. The aircraft was also docile at the low approach speeds, the second aircraft having been the one allocated to autoland development. The fourth aircraft was used by the FAA for engineering analysis as part of the certification process before it flew, the certification flight testing becoming a major part of the programme from November until completion in April 1972. Two TriStars were to be delivered to Eastern the month before certification to allow crew training and route proving, although initial crew training commenced in early October, on development aircraft.

Two of the test TriStars had uprated 42,000lb engines fitted by October 1971, with a ship set being delivered every 10 days. The flight test programme was ahead of schedule with 700hr clocked in about 290 flights. All airline guarantees would be met or exceeded and the component replacement times had been reduced by 40% below a guaranteed level set three years previously. Centre engine change had been achieved in 1hr 12min as against 2hr 45min guaranteed. In more than 70 autolands, the system performed so well that a maximum variation of 20ft from the runway centreline was recorded. Turbulence tests were flown on the gust boom-equipped first aircraft with an extended nose cone to measure accurately the speed and direction of wind gusts before they reached the aircraft.

The fourth TriStar joined the flight test programme on 24 October 1971 when it made its maiden flight of 1hr 5min from Palmdale in Eastern Airlines colours.

FAA flight trials leading to certification of the TriStar commenced on 16 November 1971. All the RB211 engines scheduled for delivery to Lock-

heed during the year had been despatched, with a further 50 due in the first six months of 1972. On 2 December the fifth and final test TriStar made its maiden flight, just as the flight test programme passed the halfway mark of 870hr flown, out of 1,700hr planned. The fifth aircraft was allocated to fly simulated airline operations and crew training, eventually due for delivery to Eastern.

A provisional airworthiness certificate was granted to the TriStar by the US FAA on 27 December 1971, two months ahead of the revised schedule. This allowed the aircraft to fly on non-revenue operations including route-proving and demonstration flights. Engine testing had continued to progress well with the 150hr flight test approval programme completed successfully. Turbine temperatures were within guarantees and the engines operated satisfactorily in freezing fog. By the end of 1971 parts construction and subassembly of the 51st TriStar had commenced at Burbank and major assembly of the 22nd aircraft had begun at Palmdale. The sixth and seventh aircraft were due to be rolled out during January 1972 with delivery to Eastern and TWA for crew training expected in March.

The TriStar icing trials proved the satisfactory operation of the ice protection system following 24hr of flight time in icing conditions off the USA and Canadian Pacific coastlines up to Alaska at altitudes between 10,000ft and 20,000ft. The RB211 engines were capable of flight idle in severe icing conditions.

Rolls-Royce continued to experience delays in certification of the RB211 engines, even beyond the February 1972 contract delivery date renegotiated with Lockheed by the new Rolls-Royce (1971). In addition to the flight test programme two testbed engines were being run at Derby on the 150hr certification type test, including 20hr at full power, one operating at a cold day thrust of 45,000lb and the other on a 22°C day at 38,000lb. The lower rating was increased by using cast instead of forged compressor blades.

By early February 1972 the TriStar test fleet had logged nearly 1,300 flight hours of the 1,670hr required for FAA certification, and the British ARB test team had started their certification studies. Testing had included rejected take-offs at the maximum take-off weight of 430,000lb. Premature take-offs were also made which involved rotation at 15kt below normal speed with the tail scraping the ground. These tests, during which excellent control was maintained, implied a high-drag condition and degradation of control properties in the engine failure case. Structural testing had simulated 12,500 fatigue flights, equivalent to 10 years of service. Static structural testing with critical members cut had been completed successfully.

In early March 1972, Rolls-Royce received from the British ARB the letter containing amendments to the provisional certification obtained on 24 February, clearing the RB211 for airline operations. This allowed thrust guarantees of 42,000lb to be set for the first year of service of the TriStar at temperatures of 66°F, increasing to 84°F after the first year following high-pressure turbine-blade modifications. Three airline standard RB211s were already flying in the function and reliability route-proving TriStar. Total run-ning time of the engines as of 5 March 1972 was 14,635hr with 7,990hr accumulated by 18 bench running engines. Flight running totalled about 1,500hr.

Full certification was granted to Rolls-Royce for the RB211-22C engine, simultaneously by the ARB and the US FAA on 22 March 1972. Nine production standard engines had been delivered to Lockheed and one RB211 was being produced every working day, with some 140 engines due for delivery in 1972.

Above:
The initial development programme for the TriStar involved the prototype and up to five early production aircraft flying in Eastern and TWA colours.

Right:
The Rolls-Royce RB211-22 engines performed well during the TriStar's flight development and certification programme, despite earlier technical problems.

On 15 April 1972 the TriStar was awarded its FAA type certificate, some five months later than originally planned, enabling passenger services to commence with the launch customers, TWA and Eastern. Despite the delay, the airlines were not too worried, as with the lull in passengers, there was adequate capacity and earlier delivery of the TriStar could have caused more empty seats to be flown around the sky. The TriStar was the first airliner to have Cat 3a, 200m altitude and 700ft runway visual range (RVR) certification of its automatic flight control system included in the initial certificate. This gave the aircraft a considerable edge over the Boeing 747 and McDonnell Douglas DC-10, since it could operate more regularly in poor weather conditions, an edge it maintained for some 15 years to the advantage of the travelling public. The TriStar was also the quietest commercial jet, as well as the most advanced at the time. Noise levels measured were 98EPNdB for take-off, 95 for side-line and 103 for approach. The regulations in FAR Part 36 limits for noise certification in the case of TriStar are 105.6, 107 and 107EPNdB respectively.

Despite the massive financial problems the TriStar had achieved its technical goals and was set to commence paying its way for the manufacturer and operators.

Above:

Although the first production TriStar N31001 was painted in TWA colours for the flight development programme, making its maiden flight on 15 February 1971, it was eventually delivered to Eastern as N301EA on 24 March 1973 after being refurbished.

Below:

The TriStar demonstrated its automatic flight system on 25 May 1972 by flying fully automatically from Palmdale to Washington, DC, including hands off take-off and an autoland.

5 Sales and Service

As has been mentioned in previous chapters, the Lockheed TriStar and the Rolls-Royce RB211 engine were launched by the major simultaneous orders by Eastern Airlines and TWA, announced in New York on 29 March 1968. Eastern Airlines orders and options covered a total of 50 aircraft and TWA needed 44. To compensate for the British engine choice, over an American equivalent, Air Holdings contracted for 30 aircraft, with options on 20 more, for sale to airlines outside the USA.

The Eastern Airlines order was valued at £358 million with deliveries of 25 aircraft due in 1972

and the remaining 25 options through 1973 and 1974. The TWA order for 44 aircraft worth £313 million was split equally in the same timetable as Eastern. The Air Holdings contract for the 30 firm orders worth £184 million was for delivery from late 1973 as capacity on the production line became available, and the options for the additional 20 aircraft, when realised, would bring the total value to £300 million.

Soon after the initial launch two more US domestic trunk route carriers joined the customer list, Delta and Northeast. The Delta order was initially for 24 aircraft worth £150 million, 12 to be

Above:
Eastern Airlines was one of the two joint launch customers for the TriStar on 29 March 1968. The second production TriStar, N301EA, first flew on 17 May 1971 and after taking part in the development programme was delivered to Eastern as N302EA on 22 May 1973.

Right:
TWA shared the launch of the TriStar with Eastern, by placing orders for 44 aircraft. L-1011-100 N31033 was one of the last aircraft for TWA, and was delivered to the airline in March 1982.

Left:
The lower deck galley gave more space for passengers on the main deck and allowed the flight attendants to prepare the meals without interruption by passengers.

Below:
Air Canada placed an order for 10 TriStars, as the first out of the Air Holdings allocation. TriStar 100 C-FTNK is an example of the type used on transatlantic services to Manchester Airport. On this aircraft the C1, C2 and C3 underfloor cargo doors are open.
Paul Francis

delivered in 1972 and the remainder in 1973. The Northeast order was for four aircraft plus four options to be delivered in 1972, in a contract worth £25 million. This brought total orders within less than one month of launch of the TriStar to 152 aircraft, worth £1,035 million, including £160 million earned by Rolls-Royce.

The airlines were keen to introduce this new technology tri-jet, with its high passenger capacity to match the expected growth in travelling numbers, and the wide bodied interior to be more attractive to the occupants. Its range flexibility was a particular advantage flying economically from US coast-to-coast nonstop, or the shorter segments such as New York to Chicago or Phoenix to Los Angeles. Seat-mile costs would be lower than any of the jets operating at the time. The TriStar would also be compatible with the Boeing 747, particularly in the use of the terminal facilities. Northeast planned to use the TriStars initially on its Boston to Florida and New York to Florida routes, with 40 first-class seats and 227 tourist-class, eventually linking Montreal, Baltimore, Washington and Philadelphia with Florida. Northeast added two more firm TriStar orders in mid-1968 bringing total sales to 174 aircraft.

In the Air Holdings contract, it was understood that Lockheed would only sell to airlines in the USA, leaving Air Holdings as the worldwide sales distributors, with the responsibility of arranging

Aerial kitchen location.

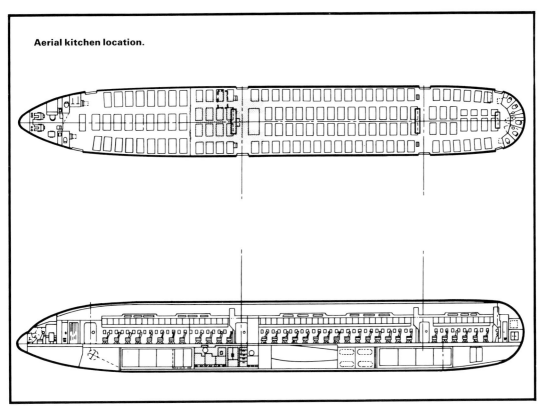

Aerial kitchen plan view.

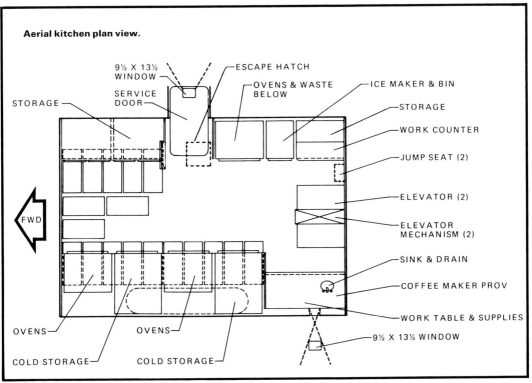

9½ X 13½ WINDOW

ESCAPE HATCH

OVENS & WASTE BELOW

ICE MAKER & BIN

SERVICE DOOR

STORAGE

STORAGE

WORK COUNTER

JUMP SEAT (2)

FWD

ELEVATOR (2)

ELEVATOR MECHANISM (2)

SINK & DRAIN

COFFEE MAKER PROV

WORK TABLE & SUPPLIES

9½ X 13½ WINDOW

OVENS

OVENS

COLD STORAGE

COLD STORAGE

any financial needs, including credit arrangements, through the City of London merchant bankers, Lazard Brothers. Overseas sales predictions by Lockheed were 175 aircraft by 1975 and could even reach 500 by 1980.

The first TriStar sale out of the Air Holdings batch was for 10 aircraft for Air Canada, ordered in December 1968 with options on nine more. This was followed in April of the same year by an order for two aircraft by the newly formed Air Jamaica, worth £12.5 million, also as part of the Air Holdings allocation, although the contract was placed with Lockheed direct. The Air Holdings order was supported by an indemnity from Rolls-Royce, and half the commitment up to a maximum of £5 million was underwritten by the British Government. If no aircraft were sold by Air Holdings, the total potential liability was estimated to be £15 million. With the sale of TriStars to Air Canada and Air Jamaica, the liability was reduced to £10 million and the British Govern-

ment received an appropriate share of the profits. Additional orders in December 1968 for lease to airlines were three aircraft for Air Finance and two for Turner & Haas.

Some ground was lost on the order book progress when Northeast Airlines decided to merge with Northwest Airlines in early 1970. Northwest already had orders for 14 long range DC-10-20s with options on a further 14. However, Northeast eventually merged with Delta on 1 April 1972.

The loss of this modest order was largely replaced by a new order when the prototype TriStar was officially rolled out at Palmdale. The first order in over a year came from Pacific Southwest Airlines (PSA) who issued a Letter of Intent for two TriStars on 1 September 1970, with reservations on three further delivery positions. PSA, the Californian airline, was the largest US intra-state carrier. The first two aircraft were planned for the high density 284nm Los Angeles-San Francisco route from 1972, with the other aircraft being delivered from 1973. The expected configuration was to be between 250 and 300

seats to cope with the heavy anticipated growth of the route over the following six years. The confirmation of the order was subject to satisfactory financial arrangements, although the airline was weathering a tight economic period, with an aircraft overcapacity at the time. The RB211 was seen as being particularly suited for the more frequent cycling of the engines, with the large number of take-offs and landings characteristic of PSA operations.

In September 1971, British & Commonwealth Shipping assumed the worldwide TriStar sales responsibilities when it increased its share of Air Holdings from 46% to a full takeover. While the players were locked in negotiations on the future of the aircraft and engine, All-Nippon Airways of Japan placed an option for six TriStars in early March 1971, but no money changed hands.

On 20 October 1971, Lockheed clarified the order situation on the TriStar. There were a total of 103 firm orders, with 46 second buys, for which non-returnable deposits had been paid. The commitment for 50 with Air Holdings still stood, but the airline had failed to meet the 1 October deadline for the progress payments on 29 of the aircraft which were unallocated to customers. Lockheed therefore reduced its previous 75 second buys accordingly.

This adjustment was only a bookkeeping exercise, since the actual order book was not affected. Air Holdings was still expected to take the aircraft as part of the RB211 offsets. The terms of the contract stipulated that if the 1 October payment was missed, Lockheed could waive the contract, retain the money already deposited until 31 July 1977, and use it to finance the production programme. Refunds would be made to Air Holdings as each of the 29 aircraft were sold, all the outstanding funds being returned by July 1977. The deposits paid by Air Holdings on the first 21 aircraft, 10 plus nine for Air Canada and one plus one for Air Jamaica, had been refunded as the airlines made their own progress payments. The Air Jamaica order was later cancelled.

Lockheed retained the responsibility for selling the aircraft with Air Holdings as a marketing partner. It appeared that it was more profitable for Air Holdings to part with the money already transferred to Lockheed for a long period, than to continue to make payments on aircraft which were not selling, the latest export order being in April 1969. The production order for 555 RB211 engines from Rolls-Royce was unaffected.

Within a few days of the Lockheed announcement, Court Line, a Luton-based British tour operator, ordered two TriStars with options on three more. The two initial aircraft were due for delivery in time for the 1973 summer season, with the optional aircraft due for delivery at the rate of one per year from 1974. Court Line became the first inclusive tour operator to order a wide-bodied jet, and the first European TriStar customer. The initial order, worth £19 million, was placed in association with Clarkson's Holidays, with which Court Line had just signed a new five-year contract providing a high utilisation.

The TriStar would give Court Line a range of up to 2,700 miles, bringing every major holiday centre in Europe, North Africa and the Eastern Mediterranean within nonstop range, and increasing the ability to boost winter utilisation. The aircraft would be 400-seat single-class aircraft in a 3-4-3 configuration, the only visible external change from the basic aircraft being a double wide door to cut down delays in passenger boarding and disembarkation. Each TriStar would be staffed by 12 cabin crew, the first aircraft being painted in an orange livery, and the second one pink. Integral air-stairs and baggage handling conveyors eased operations at remote airports without ground handling facilities. The Court Line order was finally signed on 12 August 1972 when the financial arrangements had been confirmed. Airlease International was technically the purchaser, leasing the aircraft to Court Line. The first Court Line TriStar made its maiden flight in late January 1973.

As the provisional airworthiness certificate was granted to the TriStar at the end of 1972, the PSA order was in some doubt. The reported cancellation of the two TriStars and three options was caused by a failure to agree on the renegotiated contract following the Lockheed financial crisis. PSA intended to re-evaluate the TriStar choice, and talks continued with Lockheed. The decision had been caused by a need for agreement by the end of 1972, but small deposits had already been paid at earlier dates.

The first two TriStars were handed over to Eastern and TWA at the beginning of April 1972 for crew training prior to certification in mid-April, to be ready for the start of passenger operations. Eastern in fact received the first delivery on 6 April with N306EA, and three of its captains were already qualified to fly the aircraft. This allowed Eastern to commence services from Miami on 26 April, departing at 07.00 for New York with 123 passengers. This was not an official

Left:
Special retractable airstairs were developed by Lockheed for the Court Line aircraft, to speed turnround at outstations. When retracted, it was stowed in the C2 hold, since package tour operators do not normally carry cargo.

Top right:
Eastern Airlines commenced commercial services with the TriStar flying from Miami to New York on 26 April 1972. TriStar 1 N334EA was delivered in November 1976 and is seen here at Toronto. *P. J. Birtles*

Right:
The wide-bodied interior of the proposed coach class on the TriStar, developed on the cabin mock-up had six abreast seating and meal service from both aisles.

inaugural, as the aircraft was substituted for a DC-8 and was one of the two aircraft delivered to the airline by that time.

The first TriStar was delivered to TWA for crew training in early May, to prepare for service entry on daily nonstop flights from St Louis to Los Angeles and Chicago to Los Angeles. Each TWA aircraft had a 206-seat layout. On Sunday 25 June 1972 at 17.00 TWA TriStar N31001 pushed back at St Louis at the start of the inaugural flight to Los Angeles. There was a full complement of 30 first-class passengers, and in the economy section only 10 of the 176 seats were unoccupied. For the 1,527-mile flight, some 87,000lb of fuel had been uplifted, giving a take-off weight of around 378,000lb. The take-off was entirely automatic from the point of lining up on the runway, and the whole flight was completed automatically until turning off the runway at Los Angeles. This was a remarkable achievement for the advanced avionics so early in the career of a new aircraft. The aircraft operated at 31,000ft and a cruising speed of Mach 0.87 gave a true airspeed of 520kt. Out of the total flight time of 3hr 10min, take-off to cruising altitude had been 22min, and the fuel consumption was 6,800lb per engine, per hr.

During the financial troubles, Delta had ordered five DC-10s as an insurance against a failure of the TriStar. In mid-1972, Delta confirmed its wish to have TriStars, and transferred its rights on the DC-10s to United Airlines. The arrangement was that on delivery to United, the DC-10s would be leased to Delta for about two and a half years pending delivery of sufficient TriStars and then returned to United.

British type certification of the TriStar was achieved in July 1972, culminating in about 30hr of test flying, including a fair proportion of automatic landing development work. Very few adjustments needed to be made to the aircraft, especially as the British registration authorities had been working with Lockheed for about three years in preparation.

The sales battle continued between the two tri-jets, and both were demonstrating at the same time in Japan in July 1972. The TriStar flew into Osaka and the DC-10 into Tokyo on 23 July. The next day each aircraft made two demonstration flights, followed by each aircraft changing places, flying along Japan's major trunk route. These demonstrations were part of a major world tour of both types to generate further customer

Above:
Following the major TriStar order by BEA, later to become part of British Airways, in August 1972, Eastern TriStar N305EA appeared at the SBAC display at Farnborough in September carrying BEA titles.
P. J. Birtles

interest. On completion of the Asian tour, the TriStar returned to Palmdale for maintenance in preparation for its European tour, starting in mid-August and finishing at the Farnborough Air Show. This aircraft was in the basic Eastern colours, with the airline titles changed as appropriate.

During the two sales tours, the aircraft flew 91,000 miles in 138 flights, and logged 198 flying hours. On the intensive European part of the tour, which included the Farnborough appearances, three sorties per day were averaged, carrying 8,500 passengers in 52 flights from 35 airports. Both the aircraft and engines performed well, resulting in a departure regularity of 99%.

A major sales boost came for Lockheed on 7 August 1972 from the announcement by the British Government of the approval for BEA to buy TriStars. BEA's preference for the TriStar was no secret, although it was in no hurry to place the order. The initial authority was for six standard TriStars with options on six more which could be extended-range models. The order was worth £60 million, with a further £20 million allocated to supporting service, the initial delivery being in the autumn of 1974 for services commencing in 1975. Although technically a BEA order, the selection closely involved the British Airways board in its plans for integrating BEA and BOAC. BEA could see a possible need for up to 18 aircraft by 1980, but any extended range versions would be more suited to the longer haul BOAC routes. It was also expected that BEA Airtours would use some of the TriStar capacity.

By August 1972, TriStar production was well advanced with the first aircraft for Air Canada, the 21st airframe, in assembly. Sixteen aircraft had flown, with 22 scheduled for delivery by the end of the year. The Air Canada aircraft would have a

256-passenger mixed-class layout with service entry planned on 15 February 1973.

PSA confirmed its choice of the TriStar in September 1972 by ordering five aircraft, following a successful contract renegotiation. The first two aircraft were due for delivery in the spring of 1974 and would seat between 250 and 300 passengers with a downstairs cocktail lounge as a feature. To suit the aircraft for quick turn round commuter operations on the intra-California trunk routes, a number of special features were developed including the facility to exit the maximum number of passengers through four wide doors, and the boarding of more than 100 passengers with carry-on baggage through an auxiliary entrance. The PSA order was conditional on suitable financing being available, and total sales were 113 with 51 second buys. The first PSA aircraft was delivered on 2 July 1974 and featured a lower deck entrance door into a passenger lounge.

At the time of the formal signature for the six TriStars for BEA on 26 September, the options were increased from six to 12 aircraft. Particularly useful to BEA was the low noise level of the RB211 engines which allowed round the clock operations without noise disturbance to surrounding communities, and the auto land system would provide economic and operational gains. The operations of BEA and BOAC were formally merged into British Airways (BA) on 1 April 1974.

On 28 September, TWA commenced US transcontinental daily services with the TriStar between Philadelphia and Los Angeles via Chicago. Since the introduction of the 206-seat aircraft, the operations had gradually expanded linking Chicago with Los Angeles, San Francisco and Phoenix. The US FAA gave approval in October for the TWA TriStars to operate in Category 3a weather conditions, the first aircraft to be FAA approved. The TriStar had quadruple redundancy of the major components and the operation included closing the throttles after touchdown, extending the spoilers and steering on the runway.

The All-Nippon Airways TriStar interest was confirmed in October 1972 by an initial order for six aircraft worth £55 million with deliveries due in November 1973 for use on Japan's busy domestic trunk routes. All-Nippon Airways (ANA) had had a tremendous passenger-kilometre growth rate over five years of 35% to 45%. It was the largest domestic Japanese airline with 59 routes served in 1971, 420 daily round trips and well over 28,000 seats offered daily. This was more than JAL and Toa Domestic combined on these routes. In 1970 ANA carried 7.61 million passengers and flew 4,629 million passenger-kilometres over average stage lengths of around 600km. This made it the sixth largest domestic airline in the world, with Tokyo-Osaka probably the world's second most dense air route. ANA confirmed its order by signing the contract for six TriStars in January 1973 and took out options for another 15 aircraft, bringing the overall eventual value to around £200 million.

At the same time as the ANA order was placed, the Düsseldorf-based airline LTU signed a Letter of Intent for two TriStars for delivery in May 1973 and the spring of 1975. Each aircraft would carry 330 passengers in an all-economy layout with a minimum seat pitch of 34in. LTU planned to use the aircraft on daily tourist flights from Düsseldorf to Mediterranean resorts and the Canary Islands.

Delta also increased its options by six TriStars, bringing its total commitment to 18 plus 12 aircraft. There were now 11 TriStar customers with commitment to 184 aircraft.

By November 1972, the TriStars had completed their first six months of commercial service. Both Eastern and TWA had six aircraft each in service. The RB211 engines had worked well and the predicted removal rate of the engines of 1.1 per 1,000hr had been slightly bettered. This term had been somewhat outdated by the modular construction of the engine which was maintained 'on condition', a more realistic parameter being a basic in-flight shutdown rate of 0.55 per 1,000hr. The engine entered service on an 8hr daily utilisation with 2.8hr average stage lengths with Eastern and later on 10hr daily utilisation with 3.5hr average stages with TWA. Any problems encountered with the engine were relatively minor and the cure was provided rapidly. TWA and Eastern also operated a reciprocal TriStar leasing programme, designed to spread capacity more economically between their different peak seasons.

The first Air Canada TriStar was rolled out at Palmdale in late December 1972 with delivery due by the end of January. The initial services were

planned to start on 15 February on the Toronto to Miami route for the busy winter holiday season. A month later the TriStar was due to be used on the transcontinental Montreal-Toronto-Vancouver trunk route. In addition to its 10 firm orders, Air Canada had an arrangement with the Haas-Turner finance house to share a further two TriStars with Eastern, at times to suit the two airlines' traffic peaks. The overall Air Canada requirement was seen to be for about 30 TriStars, including any long range developments.

There had however been some problems with the RB211 engines. On 28 December 1972, an Eastern Airlines TriStar suffered a complete loss of the titanium fan from the number three engine. There were no injuries to passengers or crew and the fan fell into the Atlantic. A second similar incident occurred on 10 January 1973 to the number one engine on a TWA TriStar flying from

Chicago to Los Angeles, again with no injuries, and the fan fell into the desert but was not recovered. The fan inspection period was reduced to 150 aircraft cycles, the Eastern aircraft having completed about 250 cycles were replaced by new units and some evidence of cracking was found in the discs removed from the older engines. The main concentration of the investigation was on fatigue failure of the titanium-alloy forged fan disc, allowing a number of blades to separate. At Lockheed, a flight test programme was operated with an RB211 engine fitted with strain gauges to assess stresses in flight.

After a detailed investigation on both sides of the Atlantic, Rolls-Royce announced results of the engine problem analysis. Stress levels were reduced during the material manufacture for the fan discs, all discs were spun up on additional quality control test to a rated speed before final

Above:
Also in October 1972, the Düsseldorf-based German charter operator, LTU signed a Letter of Intent for two TriStar 1s. L-1011-1 D-AERA was delivered in June 1973, but was later sold to Eastern Airlines.

inspection, disc component thickness was increased as an interim procedure, and in the long term a definitive standard disc would be developed, possibly using a new titanium alloy.

The first British-registered TriStar, named *Halcyon Days* for Court Line arrived at Luton Airport on 5 March 1973. The 400-seat aircraft was ready to commence services to Palma on 2 April. A utilisation annually of 3,000hr per aircraft was planned with these aircraft. Initial training of the two pilots and 'systems operator' for the first five or six crews was completed at Palmdale, the remainder being trained on the airline's own Redifon flight simulator.

The introduction of the Court Line TriStars brought new low levels of noise to Luton Airport and the destinations. Each TriStar could carry the equivalent of three and a half BAC One Eleven passenger loads yet made much less noise. The TriStar was permitted a full allowance of 340 night movements, even before the normal quota was divided up amongst the operators at Luton. The TriStars were concentrated on the Luton to Palma and Rimini routes, replacing BAC One Elevens, in addition to trips to Athens and North Africa. On the shorter routes economics of the TriStar were comparable to the BAC One Eleven, but over longer ranges, it became increasingly competitive. The new aircraft would allow Court Line to expand its destinations to the Caribbean, where it had hotel interests and also owned Liat, with a technical stop in the Azores. Utilisation was planned at 72hr per week for the first summer season and during the quieter winter season one aircraft could be leased out.

Due to financial troubles with Clarksons Holidays, the parent company, Shipping Industrial Holdings, sold a controlling 85% of its holiday tour subsidiary for a nominal sum to Court Line. Some 40% of Court Line business was generated by the five-year Clarksons contract and Court Line found its marketing expertise useful. The option on the third TriStar might be deferred and the other two options could either be cancelled or delayed. The second Court Line TriStar, *Halcyon Breeze*, was delivered to Luton nonstop from Palmdale on 3 May 1973. This 5,500-mile great circle route was the longest flight by a TriStar to date and was flown automatically from start of take-off to touchdown.

In its first year of commercial airline service, TriStar carried more than 1.3 million passengers and covered more than 2,000 million passenger-miles. Eastern, TWA, Air Canada and Court Line accumulated nearly 30,000 flying hours on more than 11,000 revenue earning flights. Twenty-five TriStars had been delivered, about a dozen behind schedule, but future deliveries included the first for LTU, Delta and ANA, all in 1973. In fact, the first LTU aircraft was delivered on 29 May 1973 to Düsseldorf.

The first Delta TriStar, N701DA was rolled out at Palmdale ready for its first flight on 7 September 1973 and was delivered to the airline on 3 October. Services commenced in December covering New York, Philadelphia, Atlanta, Houston, Miami, New Orleans and Tampa.

Meanwhile, in September 1973, ANA took up eight of its TriStar options worth over £120

million, bringing its firm orders for the type to 14 aircraft. Another two were confirmed in October 1974. Although ANA was primarily a domestic operator, with the arrival of the TriStars, the airline planned weekly charter flights between Tokyo and Manila in the Philippines. ANA ordered pylon attachments for four of its TriStars to enable them to ferry spare RB211 engines. The pylon was attached to the right-hand wing between the engine and the fuselage.

In October, the European division of British Airways increased its TriStar order by three. This brought the total to nine, with a further nine on option.

The fuel crisis starting in late 1973 brought further financial problems to Lockheed, largely as the result of deferment of orders and options due to an overcapacity with the airlines. Eastern Airlines deferred the delivery of nine TriStars, a subsequent slow down in production being a very costly exercise. Lockheed had healthy orders and options for 199 TriStars, of which 56 had been delivered up to the end of 1973. Plans allowed for 35 to be delivered in each of 1974 and 1975. The lack of cash would affect any long-range developments, restricting the overall market. If arrangements could not be made with the banks, a possible alternative was a merger with another

Above:

Cathay Pacific signed a Letter of Intent for two TriStars, with options on two more in March 1974. These were the first aircraft fitted with a centre-section fuel tank. To help supplement its fleet, TriStar 1 N316EA was leased from Eastern in March 1980. *Cathay Pacific*

Right:

Cathay Pacific acquired Eastern TriStar N325EA and registered it VR-HHY for delivery in July 1978. It shares the Hong Kong apron with VR-HHV and VR-HHK. *Cathay Pacific*

company, talks later being held with Hughes and Textron.

Lockheed's cash flow problems were eased by Delta, TWA and ANA asking for a total of seven TriStars to be delivered early. With the worsening fuel crisis, rationing allocations to 90% of that used in 1973 in some cases, the fuel efficient RB211-powered TriStars were more economical than the aircraft they were replacing.

In March 1974, Cathay Pacific signed a Letter of Intent for two TriStars plus two options. These were the first aircraft fitted with a centre-section fuel tank and the maximum take-off weight was increased to 46,000lb. Later in the same month, Saudia ordered two TriStars for delivery in mid-1975, with options on a further three aircraft. The order was for L-1011-100s fitted with increased wing fuel tankage, but without the centre section tanks specified by Cathay Pacific. Take-off weight of Saudia's aircraft was to be increased by 20,000lb to 450,000lb and they were able to carry 259 passengers over a range of 4,000 miles.

Court Line's borrowings during the early part of 1974 had been unexpectedly high, and in June, after a dramatic fall in its share prices, trading in the shares was halted on the London Stock Exchange. Talks were held between the company, its bankers and the British Government to try to avert a crisis, which would not only affect Court Line, but the major tour operators, Clarksons and Horizon. The difficulties were largely caused by holiday bookings reduced by a third over 1973. Also the depression in the tanker operating market and lack of success in the group's shipbuilding and Caribbean investments all contributed to the cash flow problems. To recover the situation, the British Government proposed nationalisation of 16 Court Line companies involved in ship building and repair, making available £15 million to finance the remainder of the group.

In mid-1974 British Airways was well advanced in its preparations for the first of its nine TriStar 1s, all of which featured a 104in by 68in forward freight door large enough to accept standard 125in by 88in containers. The preparations were costing around £36 million, which was more than one-third of the purchase price of the aircraft. British Airways engineers had liaised closely with Court Line on the introduction of its two TriStars, which helped in the provisioning plans. An engine test cell was built capable of handling engines of over 80,000lb thrust and capable of adaptation to any of the large engines. Redifon supplied a flight simulator and was complemented by an engineering simulator capable of reproducing 385 engineering faults. For additional training, a cockpit procedures simulator, systems trainers and passenger cabin mock-up were ordered, the latter for cabin crew training. Ground support equipment had to be bought and the departure gates had to be adapted at Heathrow. Lockheed had already trained 53 maintenance personnel and 28 aircrew.

The first three BA TriStars were due for delivery towards the end of October 1974, allowing first commercial services to start a month later. First points to be served were Malaga, Palma, Madrid and Brussels, increasing to Paris Orly, in December. British Airways' first TriStar, G-BBAE,

made its maiden flight from Palmdale on 3 September 1974. The aircraft was configured with 20 first-class seats and 300 economy seats. It was delivered to Heathrow on 21 October 1974 but service entry was delayed by industrial action.

On Thursday 15 August 1974 the Court Line Group announced that it was going into liquidation, stranding some 49,000 holidaymakers at their destinations. Fortunately a £3.3 million bond had been lodged with the Association of British Travel Agents, allowing a number of other British airlines to mount a recovery operation. The two TriStars and nine BAC One-Elevens operated by Court Line were grounded. Despite the Government payment for the shipbuilding interests, it soon became apparent that, at the best, operations could only continue until the end of the holiday season in September. Even this proved impossible after an examination of the company's books. Both the TriStars, which were leased by Court Line, were stored at Luton, becoming a regular landmark, until they were flown to Palmdale and later refurbished for sale to Cathay Pacific in the autumn of 1977.

ANA had to ground its six TriStars on 4 September 1974 due to two occasions when two engines were shut down on approach to Tokyo. The problem was found to be oil loss due to cracks in a pressure casing around a drilled oil-scavenger aperture. Services were gradually restarted on 8 September by changing the faulty modules for a later standard model. This relatively minor problem did not stop ANA signing an agreement for seven more TriStars in September 1974, conditional upon the Japanese Government allowing wide-bodied aircraft into Osaka Airport. Even without Osaka, at least two more TriStars were required.

The first order for what became known as the L-1011-200 was for two long-range TriStars from Saudia on 19 September 1974. The last of what was then a total of four aircraft was due for delivery in 1977, powered by the uprated RB211-524 engines. These developed 48,000lb thrust each, an increase of 6,000lb over the earlier engine. The remaining three aircraft were to be retrofitted with the new engines making them all to the -200 standard. The new aircraft were expected to have a range of 4,700 miles with full reserves which gave it a transatlantic capability.

Delta, having introduced the TriStars to replace its leased DC-10s, converted three of its 12 options into firm orders in November 1974, bringing their total orders to 21 aircraft. Later in the same month, British Airways increased its order by six more standard TriStars, bringing its total orders to 15. Also, Gulf Air signed a contract for four extended-range TriStar 100s, in December 1974, the first two to be delivered in January and February 1976. The contract included four options. These aircraft had 18,000lb of additional fuel in the wing centre-section and a maximum take-off weight of 466,000lb. They were initially fitted with RB211-22B engines, but the options were open for a later retrofit of more powerful engines.

During late December 1974 and early January 1975, British Airways carried out a series of proving flights with the three TriStars delivered to

the airline. This cleared the aircraft for the first London to Paris service to start on 12 January, followed by Brussels and Madrid the next day, and Malaga and Palma soon after. With five aircraft in service by the end of February, TriStars were phased into sorties to Amsterdam, Tel Aviv, Faro, Alicante and Athens in time to meet the start of the summer schedules on 1 April.

The continuing fuel crisis in 1975 and a recession in the air transport industry particularly affected the US markets. Both Eastern and TWA had an excess of capacity equal to about four TriStars each and in March PSA grounded its two TriStars, replacing them with Boeing 727-200s following a 10% decline in traffic. The TriStars were reintroduced in June. LTU purchased an Eastern TriStar in July 1975. Saudia's first TriStar, an extended-range L-1011-100 was delivered in July 1975 ready for services to start on 15 August.

After more than a year on the ground at Luton, the ex-Court Line TriStar G-BAAA flew on

Above:
Gulf Air signed a contract for four extended-range TriStar 100s in December 1974. Its first aircraft G-BDCW first flew on 16 December 1975, but was converted to a series 200 and delivered as A 40-TW in January 1976.

Below:
Saudia's first TriStar 100 was delivered in July 1975 ready for services to start on 15 August. TriStar 1 HZ-AHE was originally allocated to TWA, but delivered to Saudia in February 1976. It was later converted to a L-1011-100 and then a L-1011-200.

28 August 1975, followed soon after by the other aircraft. The owner of the aircraft, Airlease International was renewing the certification of the aircraft. Both aircraft departed Luton for Palmdale in late November 1975 for updating and eventual disposal.

Left:
The Lockheed L-1011 full flight simulator duplicated all normal flight attitudes, reducing significantly the time and cost of pilot training.

Below:
Gulf Air took delivery of the first of its luxuriously-appointed TriStars at the end of January 1976 ready for the Bahrain to London services to commence on 1 April. L-1011-200 A 40-TY was delivered on 5 June 1976, the aircraft carrying British registration on the early operations. *P. J. Birtles*

Below right:
After lease with Aero Peru, the ex-PSA aircraft were sold to Worldways of Canada. TriStar 100 N10114 became C-GIFE and was delivered on 20 June 1985. The entry door to the lower lounge can be seen outlined in black.

Gulf Air took delivery of its first TriStar at the end of January 1976, to prepare for the start of its Bahrain to London service in April. These aircraft had the most luxurious layout of any airliners in service, with only 171 economy-class and 40 first-class seats. Also in January, Delta increased its order by one TriStar, to a total of 22 aircraft, this being the first sale for over one year, none having been achieved in 1975. However, Cathay Pacific cancelled two of its options in February and two new TWA aircraft were sold straight off the production line to Saudia.

On 17 March 1976, Gulf Air demonstrated its Golden Falcon TriStar, G-BDCX, to the press and travel agents with a 40min flight from London to Amsterdam. This was one of two aircraft delivered with two more arriving in May and June. The seating was plush and roomy, the first-class seats being at 40in pitch and the economy-class at 34in pitch. The centre pair of seats in the first-class cabin could be swivelled to face a table, forming a four-place conference or dining area. There was no surcharge for the extra luxury, the long-term passenger attraction being expected to justify the investment in all the extra fittings. The introduction of the TriStars doubled Gulf Air's capacity from London to the Gulf, the major competitor at the time being the newly introduced Concorde. The regular Gulf Air TriStar services were inaugurated on 1 April 1976.

Lockheed's financial troubles still plagued the TriStar programme, aggravated by the fuel crisis giving a significant drop in demand for new aircraft, despite their greater fuel productivity. To make a profit, it was necessary to sell 300 of the basic L-1011-1 version, but the decrease in production rate gave less efficient use of the tooling. Programme costs were also increased by even modest developments of the existing airframe. In April 1976, firm TriStar orders stood at 157 plus 50 options, covering the three variants

then available, the standard L-1011-1, the extended-range L-1011-100 and long-range RB211-524-powered L-1011-200. Lockheed had delivered 127 TriStars, but the 1976 rate was expected to be between nine and 12 aircraft, due to the paucity in orders which was one option confirmed by Delta. Eight of the 30 aircraft backlog were for British Airways, which needed its deliveries spread evenly up to 1982. The TriStar was not unique in its lack of sales, as the medium-range DC-10-10 had not achieved any sales over the same period, but at least a long-range version could already be supplied and more DC-10s had been sold overall. Lockheed had not achieved the conditions required for a merger with Textron to inject additional investment cash, the earlier Hughes bid having also lapsed. The Lockheed bribes scandal reported widely at the time had not helped credibility in a market place where only the Airbus was collecting orders.

Orders for new aircraft were not encouraged by the number of second-hand aircraft available. The first two PSA aircraft were grounded at the airline's base and the other three remained undelivered. The two ex-Court Line aircraft were still at Palmdale, and Eastern had disposed of three of its current fleet and was interested in selling more, either from service or off the production line. TWA was disposing of aircraft from the production line and ANA threatened to cancel three deposit-paid options.

At the same time as the start of the Gulf Air TriStar operations from Bahrain to London, British Airways Overseas Division began to replace its VC10s and Boeing 707s on the services to Abu Dhabi, Dubai, Dhahran and Kuwait. This was achieved with two TriStar L-1011-1s on a three-year transfer from the European Division. The BA TriStars were not as luxurious as the Gulf Air aircraft, but had been configured with 38 first-class seats and 202 economy-class. The use

of these TriStars helped utilise the excess capacity experienced by the European Division; although the range was on the L-1011-1 limits with the possibility of technical stops on hot days. Whereas the problem with much of the world's airline routes was overcapacity, the Gulf routes had an embarrassingly rapid growth, the BA share having grown to 45% of the market, although the TriStars were not used to compete with Concorde to Bahrain.

The first signs of the buoyant Middle East market were apparent to Lockheed, when on 25 May 1976, after 18 months with only one TriStar sale, Saudia ordered three more RB211-524-engined L-1011-200s for delivery starting in September 1977. The value of this order was $98.6 million, and the two ex-TWA TriStars were to be re-engined with the newer Rolls-Royce engine. However, the order for new TriStars was reduced to two aircraft less than two months later due to a revision of fleet requirements.

To give the TriStar a transatlantic capability, Air Canada commenced modification of three of its aircraft to L-1011-100 standard to increase the take-off weight by 36,000lb and to make available the centre section fuel tank capacity of 19,000lb of fuel. This extended the range with 257 passengers by 900 miles. Routes to be served were from Toronto and Montreal to London, Frankfurt and Paris. The first of the three Air Canada TriStars retrofitted to the L-1011-100 standard commenced transatlantic operations at the end of April 1977. The range was increased to 3,660nm and the gross weight rose to 466,000lb for a modest increase in empty weight of 1,400lb. With the RB211 thrust remaining the same, the field length was increased from 8,350ft to 11,200ft. Air Canada also fitted duplicate Litton Inertial Navigation Systems (INS) to the three converted TriStars to assist on the long over-water navigation. TWA followed in late 1977 by converting four of its 30 L-1011-1s to the -100 configuration, with 256 seats, and more conversions followed to allow transatlantic services to start in the spring of 1978.

By the middle of 1976, the first signs of the move out of the world depression were appearing. Airlines were beginning to see a passenger growth returning and could consider expanding their fleets again. However, one of Lockheed's problems was the stock of hardly used bargain TriStars awaiting a new owner. An encouraging sign was the confirmation in August 1976 of two options by Delta for delivery in May and December 1978.

In October 1976, the German airline, LTU, came to an agreement with Lockheed to return its two TriStar L-1011-1s, and buy the three TriStar L-1011-1s built for PSA but never delivered. This would give LTU the advantage of a high density layout common to all three aircraft, instead of adding a new aircraft to a later standard of modification, without full commonality with the earlier two. The first of the three new TriStars was delivered to LTU in mid-March 1977 ready for the airline to become the first regular transatlantic TriStar operator on 4 April. The services were advanced booking charter flights between Düsseldorf and New York. The LTU aircraft featured the lower deck passenger lounge as specified by PSA and had a door with air-stairs fitted for lower deck entry just forward of the wing leading edge. The second new TriStar was delivered in May and the third in December 1977. TriStar No 3 was cleared to the 466,000lb maximum take-off weight of the L-1011-100, but without the extra fuel capacity. LTU had no interest in carrying freight, so the extra capacity of the lower deck lounge would allow 330 passengers to be carried, nine abreast at a 34in pitch. Triple INS were fitted to assist on the long over-water flights with Omega added later.

Delta confirmed a further option for a TriStar in February 1977, with five options still remaining. This brought the total Delta fleet to 25 TriStars in service by the end of 1978. Two more were ordered in August 1977 for delivery in 1979. In October 1978, Delta ordered five more standard L-1011-1 TriStars with options on a further 15 aircraft. The aircraft on order were for delivery in 1980 to 1981 and the options covered delivery positions between 1982 and 1984. This was the largest order for the TriStar for over four years.

ANA confirmed its options for three more TriStars in April 1977 bringing its total fleet size of the type to 20 aircraft. Saudia increased its order in May 1977 by two L-1011-200s for delivery in late 1978, bringing its total fleet to 10 aircraft, the first -200 having been delivered to the airline on 27 May. In May 1978 Saudia further increased its fleet of TriStars to 13, by ordering three more aircraft.

In January 1979, British Airways ordered its first two TriStar 200s for delivery in March 1980. These aircraft, powered by the RB211-524 engines, were initially to supplement the similarly-powered TriStar 500s on the Gulf route, releasing the TriStar 1s back to the European Division. In February, a new Washington-based airline, Trans CaribAir, was reported to have ordered one TriStar 200, with two more on option. The first aircraft was due for delivery in June 1980 for operations between New York and Puerto Rico. This operation did not materialise and the orders lapsed.

Gulf Air ordered two TriStar -200s in August 1979 to add to its fleet of four -100s. The new aircraft were scheduled for delivery in February and March 1981 and were fitted with the Flight Management System (FMS) similar to those offered on the later -500s.

British Airways ordered six more TriStar -200s in September 1979 with deliveries commencing six months later. This order was valued at £127 million and brought BA's total TriStar commitment to 23 aircraft. At this time Lockheed claimed in excess of 300 TriStar sales, consisting of 270 firm orders and 71 options. In a period of two months, Lockheed had sold 23 TriStars worth £560 million, including 14 to unannounced customers.

Delta Air Lines continued to top up its TriStar fleet when it converted two options to firm orders for L-1011-1s in March 1980 for delivery in December 1981 and January 1982. This brought Delta's total to 32 TriStars in service, eight on firm order and a further 13 options. Gulf Air added a seventh TriStar with an order in the spring of 1980. Delta added another TriStar in July 1980, a further one in the following month, another in November and one more in early 1981. Two more options were converted into firm orders for TriStar 1s by Delta in April 1981 for delivery in April and May 1983. Delta planned to have 44 of the type in service by mid-1983, with 10 still scheduled for delivery over the following two years and seven options remaining.

Many of the TriStars are still in service with their original operators confirming Lockheed's original design philosophy of producing a high technology quality airliner which would stand the test of time. It is a highly reliable aircraft which generates good revenue for the airlines, even if it was not profitable for the manufacturer. Lockheed continue to support the 240-plus aircraft still in operation providing product improvements to further enhance reliability, ease of maintenance, performance and safety. Probably the major reason the aircraft was not more successful, was the lack of a complementary long-range version early in the programme available to compete with the DC-10, largely due to a lack of sufficient funding. The TriStar was probably launched on too low an investment level and also failed to gain a place in the major ATLAS and KSSU groups of European airlines which would have helped to have ensured its long-term financial success.

Below:
American Trans Air is a frequent charter operator from the USA into Europe, Gatwick being its London terminal. Eight L-1011-1s were acquired from Delta in 1985. *P. J. Birtles*

6 TriStar 500 Sales

After a highly competitive sales battle between the Boeing 747, McDonnell Douglas DC-10 and the Lockheed TriStar, British Airways announced in August 1976 its decision to place a launch order worth £140 million for the long range TriStar 500. To secure this order, Lockheed allowed British Airways to convert its remaining six options into firm orders for the long range, short body variant, but an additional six options were also placed for the TriStar 500. Four of the aircraft were due for delivery in 1979, metal having already been cut, and the other two the following year. The new aircraft was ideally suited to replace the noisy and inefficient Boeing 707s and Douglas DC-8s on the long range, low passenger capacity routes worldwide.

The most obvious market area was with the existing TriStar customers due to the commonality of operation and engineering, and many of them had large fleets of the early jet airliners due for replacement. Lockheed predicted a market for up to 244 TriStar 500s by 1985. The British Airways order also signalled the demise of the DC-10-30R, a long range variant powered by Rolls-Royce RB211-524 engines, which would have killed any prospects for the launch of a long range TriStar.

The BA TriStar 500s were to be configured with 18 first-class and 217 economy-class seats. The airline ordered the TriStar 500 for its long thin transatlantic routes from London to Philadelphia, Detroit and the West Coast destinations. The new aircraft would operate to the Caribbean and replace the European Division TriStar 200s on the Gulf routes.

After a long delay in gaining any significant TriStar sales, Delta Air Lines, one of the largest

Below:
Delta became the second L-1011-500 customer in January 1978 for its newly approved Atlanta to London (Gatwick) service. Delta is now a regular operator into Gatwick of all the versions of the TriStar. *P. J. Birtles*

operators of the aircraft, ordered two TriStar 500s in January 1978 for its newly approved Atlanta to London route. Delivery of these aircraft was due in mid-1979 and a further three options had been taken for delivery from 1981. While awaiting delivery of the new aircraft, Delta leased a pair of TWA TriStar 100s, operating at a reduced pay-load. Services commenced into Gatwick on 1 May 1978, the leased TriStar 100s having 24 first-class seats and 238 economy-class. The performance of the leased TriStars was improved by fitting the RB211-524 engines, bringing the aircraft up to the -200 standard. A third TriStar 500 was ordered in March 1979, and the first was delivered in September 1979.

In April 1978, the -500 TriStar gained further momentum with an order for 12 aircraft plus 14 options from Pan Am powered by the Rolls-Royce RB211-524 engines. This order had been a long drawn out battle, particularly for Rolls-Royce, as initially Pan Am had insisted on Pratt & Whitney JT9D engines to give commonality with its 747 fleet. The Pan Am aircraft were equipped with extended wingtips and active ailerons to improve the ride and fuel efficiency. A new FMS reduced fuel burn and engine maintenance costs. The first aircraft was due for delivery in February 1980 with services starting in April on selected South American and transatlantic routes. The

TriStar 500 replaced Pan Am's Boeing 707s and was selected after a hard battle with the DC-10-30 and Boeing 747SP. The overall value of the deal was £250 million.

In September 1978, Lockheed signed a memor-andum of understanding with Aero Peru for the purchase of a single TriStar 500 for delivery in 1981. As a stopgap, one of the former PSA TriStars was leased to the carrier, the two specially configured aircraft having proved difficult to sell. At the same time, British West Indian Airways (BWIA) gained permission from its government to order two TriStar 500s, but no contract had been signed. Two options were included, the total value being $85 million, and the first of an eventual fleet of four TriStar 500s was delivered in January 1980. The two options were confirmed in September 1980 for delivery in late 1981 and the middle of 1982.

The first BA TriStar 500 was rolled out officially at Palmdale on 12 October 1978, prior to the

commencement of the type development flying involving two aircraft in 530 flying hours. The programme included full performance and handling trials, with high speed flutter checks, stalls and rejected take-offs. The maiden flight was on 16 October, one month ahead of schedule, and the aircraft was airborne for 2hr 30min. Later the same day, it made its second flight of a similar duration, carrying out flutter checks, stall approaches, speedbrake evaluation and autoland checks.

On completion of its development and certification programme, the first TriStar 500 was delivered to British Airways on 30 April 1979. This aircraft was in fact the third in the order, G-BFCC, while the first two aircraft were being refurbished by Lockheed following the flight testing. Services commenced between Heathrow and Abu Dhabi in May with extensions to Singapore in June when the fleet had grown to three aircraft. By the time they were delivered, the aircraft had been reconfigured with 30 first-class seats and 202 economy. The new aircraft were expected to represent a fuel saving of £1 million per year over

existing aircraft. The FMS held the aircraft speed to within one knot of its preselected cruising speed, by allowing the aircraft to rise and sink gradually through a 100ft deep height band. On arrival, the '-500' was powered by RB211-524B engines, giving an improved thrust of 50,000lb. On the delivery flight of 12hr from Palmdale to Heathrow, the aircraft was flown fully automatically from 1,000ft altitude after take-off, until the approach to London.

As part of its 10-year fleet renewal programme, Air Canada ordered six TriStar 500s in April 1979, with options on a further nine aircraft. The initial order was worth about £125 million, and deliveries started in 1981. The aircraft supplied were the definitive -500 with active controls and RB211-524B4 engines, which had the same thrust as the '-524Bs', but a 4.5% improvement in cruise specific fuel consumption. The 244-seat Air Canada TriStar 500s were planned for the long haul transatlantic routes.

In May 1979, LTU added two TriStar 500s to its future fleet for delivery in March and November 1980. The new aircraft were for use on the long

haul services from Düsseldorf to New York, Los Angeles, the Caribbean, Thailand and Sri Lanka. The value of the order was a very competitive £34 million and it brought total sales of the '-500' to 32 aircraft with 31 on option, and sales of all types of TriStar to 216 plus 76 on option. The LTU aircraft were configured in an all-economy 276-seat layout and fitted with extended wingtips, active controls, FMS and the '-524B4' engines.

TAP-Air Portugal became a new customer for the TriStar in September 1979, with an order for three '-500s' and options on two more. Just as the airline was ready to sign the order, having obtained the necessary financial package, the Portuguese Government refused to give approval for the acquisition of the TriStar. Due to heavy losses over the previous two years, the government felt that the carrier's weak financial state did not justify a major fleet expansion. The management was given 60 days to present a financial restructuring capable of making the airline viable within five years. This programme was approved by the Government allowing talks to reopen with Lockheed. However, industrial

action in mid-1980 stopped negotiations again, although contacts were maintained with Lockheed. The order was finally confirmed in October 1980. The first of these aircraft was delivered in November 1982, the options being confirmed in August 1981 to make a total fleet of five TriStar 500s.

The first Pan Am '-500' made its maiden flight from Palmdale on 16 November 1979 commencing a two-aircraft flight test programme of 330 flying hours to obtain FAA certification of the extended wingtips and active controls. Pan Am's first scheduled service into London-Gatwick Airport was in July 1980, when a TriStar 500 arrived after a flight from Guatemala, Mexico City and Houston.

At the end of 1979 Alia, the Jordanian airline, ordered five TriStar 500s worth some £142 million. Four more aircraft were to be added later, plus one '-500' for the Jordanian Royal flight. The TriStars were for the European and transatlantic routes.

The last airline customer for the TriStar was Air Lanka which announced its intention to order two

Above:
At the same time that Alia added four TriStar 500s to its fleet, one JY-HKJ was also ordered for the Jordanian Royal Flight. This aircraft is maintained regularly by Marshall of Cambridge (Engineering).
Marshall of Cambridge (Engineering) Ltd

'-500s' with options on two more in March 1980. These TriStars were powered by the RB211-524B4 engines and featured all the refinements including extended wingtips and active controls. The -500s replaced leased 707s on the long haul routes to Europe. The total value of the order was some £100 million. Air Lanka also leased a number of the earlier standard of aircraft, buying two from ANA in March 1981.

The six BA TriStar 500s were retrofitted with extended wingtips and active controls to overcome a shortfall in fuel consumption. Provision had not been made originally on these early '-500s' for the retrofit modification, which resulted in a longer downtime than expected. FAA approval had already been achieved on 1 April 1980. The first conversion was delivered to BA at the end of 1980. The modifications also included changing the RB211-524B engines for the fuel efficient '-524B2' to restore a shortfall in cruise fuel consumption which was below brochure performance. The wingtip extensions added 9ft to the overall span, and the aileron span was increased accordingly. These wingspan extensions increased aspect ratio and as a result reduced the induced drag, allowing the wing to support a given weight with less drag. This drag reduction gave an estimated 2.5% saving in specific fuel consumption. The active ailerons eliminate the larger bending moment which the wing would otherwise experience. The active control system (ACS) detected when an extra load was about to be applied to the wing as a result of a manoeuvre or wind gust, and moved the aileron slightly upwards to reduce lift near the wingtips. In the case of a manoeuvre, the extra lift required was generated inboard, where there was no significant increase in wing bending moment. In a gust, the extra lift was destroyed, because it was not needed. In addition to improving fuel consumption, the passengers experienced a smoother ride in turbulence, and the fatigue life of the aircraft was extended.

The first TriStar 500 for Air Canada was rolled out at the end of 1980 for delivery in February. The aircraft with seating for 246 passengers was for use on non stop services between western Canada and Europe. Eventually only the six on firm order were taken, with the cancellation of the nine options.

With the confirmation of the Air Portugal order in October 1980, further sales only were made occasionally for aircraft to top up the Delta fleet. Some of the earlier operators were offering a few of their aircraft on the second-hand market, and the launch of the new generation wide bodied twin-engined airliners in the Airbus family and the Boeing 767s made further sales of the TriStar more and more unlikely. In the spring of 1981, it was being suggested that TriStar production may

have to be cut to reduce continuing losses on the programme. The first quarter loss on the TriStar programme in 1981 was £15 million, an increase over the same period in the previous year. The order backlog was for 44 aircraft, with 18 TriStars to be produced in 1981, but not all were sold. By scrapping TriStar production, Lockheed would become significantly more profitable, after writing off the cancellation costs. The company therefore set a limit that production would cease if less than 10 aircraft were produced in a year.

Amongst prospective customers for the '-500' was Air-India, which placed an initial order for the type in mid-1981 to replace its 707 fleet. This order was valued at £90 million with deliveries commencing in February 1983, the airline planning to acquire eventually seven or eight TriStars. This order was never confirmed.

Finally, in December 1981 Lockheed decided to cease production of the TriStar in 1984, reducing significantly the market for the Rolls-Royce RB211-524 turbofan. The decision to end TriStar production was based on the depressed commercial aircraft market which was not expected to improve before 1986. To maintain a reasonable level of business there would need to have been a sustained high rate of production of at least 24 aircraft per year from 1985 to 1990, but the expected market did not look good enough to achieve these levels.

There were still firm orders for 21 TriStars, the last for delivery in 1984, and about 40 options. Lockheed would produce any of the outstanding options, providing they were confirmed by the

Above:
Air Lanka suffered an overcapacity due to a drop in passenger demand caused by the military unrest in Sri Lanka and disposed of its 747s and leased two L-1011-500s to British Airways. Air Lanka 4RULA became G-BLUS. *Air Lanka*

middle of 1982. A total of $400 million was written off after taxes to cover the closedown of the line. Total losses on the TriStar amounted to nearly $2,500 million, including the final write-off costs.

The overall order book at the end of 1981 claimed 250 TriStars ordered with 218 in service. In the Americas, Eastern operated 26 L-1011-1s, TWA 34 -1s and -100s, Delta 37, of all types, with seven options, Pan Am 12 -500s, Air Canada 18, of all variants, Aero Peru two -100s and BWIA four -500s. In Europe BA has 23 of all variants, Air Portugal five '-500s' on order and LTU seven, of all variants in service. In the Middle East, Air Lanka has four TriStars in service or on order, Alia had commitments to five aircraft, Gulf Air operated eight aircraft, Saudia had a fleet of 17 and Air India still had an order for three -500s. Alia's fleet eventually grew to nine '-500s', plus the Jordanian Royal Flight, helping to replace the Air India order. In Asia, ANA operated 19 L-1011-1s and Cathy Pacific operated 11 TriStars. These totals allowed for three aircraft lost in accidents, the original prototype, one stored ex-PSA aircraft, and the final sale to the Algerian Government of one '-500', making an overall total of 250 aircraft.

7 Developments

The main aim of Lockheed in the proposed developments of the basic TriStar, was to achieve a long-range aircraft with a high level of commonality in operation and training. The major competitor was McDonnell Douglas which had already produced the long-range DC-10-30 to complement its initial design, but Lockheed was restrained from matching the competition due to the serious financial troubles. All that could be achieved effectively was to take advantage of the normal development growth of thrust of the RB211 engine, allowing the TriStar to increase its range by carrying a greater load of fuel.

The original TriStar long-range proposals went back to 1969 when Lockheed offered the L-1011-8.4 powered by three 52,200lb thrust Rolls-Royce RB211-56 engines. This version was to be capable of carrying up to 280 passengers, 28 first-class and 252 tourist-class over distances of 5,925 miles. Maximum take-off weight was to be 575,000lb and the main undercarriage was to have six wheels on each of the main legs to distribute the load more evenly. Wing area was to be increased by 20% over the basic aircraft, to a total of 3,456sq ft. The fuselage length was to be stretched by 40in to 182ft 8in and further development was expected with anticipated thrust growth of the engines. The cost of developing this version of the TriStar was estimated to be about £50 million, with another £60 million for the uprated engines.

A further growth in the long-range TriStar was announced in January 1970, aimed primarily at the European ATLAS group of airlines. The gross weight had increased by some 20,000lb and power would come from three RB211-56 engines of 53,500lb thust each, for service entry in 1973. These proposals were shelved with the financial problems.

The initial L-1011-1 TriStar was offered at a gross weight of 409,000lb based on a RB211 thrust of 40,600lb. When the engine thrust increased to 42,000lb on test, the TriStar gross weight was increased to 426,000lb.

In early 1971, with the financial package approved by the US Government, Lockheed was again proposing an extended range TriStar using the natural growth of the standard RB211 engine. A range of 4,000nm was planned with a load of 270 passengers.

In February 1972, Lockheed was proposing the L-1011-2 which would need a launch base of three major customers. The costs would be less than the earlier L-1011-8.4 as there would be no changes in dimensions over the standard aircraft, but overall strengthening would be required and would add about 5,000lb to the structural weight. Range was to be 4,000nm and the gross weight would increase to 466,000lb. Strong efforts were made to sell this modest improvement during 1972 mainly to existing customers.

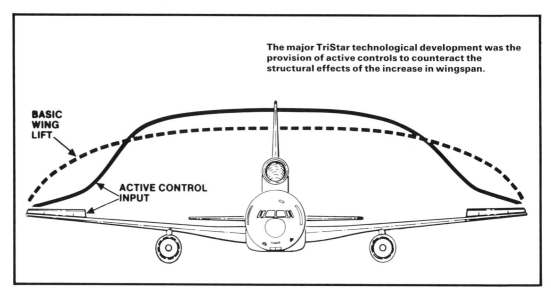

The major TriStar technological development was the provision of active controls to counteract the structural effects of the increase in wingspan.

BASIC WING LIFT

ACTIVE CONTROL INPUT

A 'BiStar' was even studied in 1972 as a twin RB211-22X powered 200 to 250 seater with Japan as full partners in the project. The aircraft would have a reduced area wing and a gross weight of 276,000lb. Seat/mile costs would be comparable with the TriStar with aircraft/mile cost 20% to 25% lower. Development costs estimated at $290 million would need to have been approved by the US Government.

When the British Government announced its agreement for BEA to order TriStars on 7 August 1972, approval was also given for the start of develoment of the RB211-24 engine, to develop 45,000lb thrust for the extended range version of the TriStar, the L-1011-2. Development costs of the engine were estimated to be £31 million. The new airframe/engine combination was expected to give a payload/range performance between the the long-range DC-10-30 and the standard TriStar. The L-1011-2 would have a full transatlantic capability in all weather conditions, making the aircraft attractive to existing customers. The new engine, known in its preproduction form as the RB211-24, but in its production form as the RB211-524, would have a maximum commonality and interchangeability with the RB211-22B, an improved specific fuel consumption, minimum weight increase, service entry by 1975 and further thrust development potential up to 50,000lb. These improvements were to be achieved by refinements to the existing engine including reduced operating temperatures: a new fan with a slightly reduced bypass ratio, but with the same diameter as the '-22B' and an increase in mass flow. The new fan blades were not to be made of carbon fibre, despite continuing research in this material. This engine was proposed not only for the L-1011-2, but a higher-capacity L-1011-3, and the 'BiStar'. With a larger fan, RB211 developments could produce 55,000lb thrust, but it would virtually be a complete redesign.

Further details emerged in April 1973 of the L-1011-2, go-ahead for which was conditional upon sufficient airline interest. Maximum take-off weight was increased to 51,000lb over the basic aircraft, to 488,000lb. Some 7,000lb of this was accounted for by the structural strengthening and changes to equipment. Range at Mach 0.82 with full reserves and carrying 273 passengers was estimated at 4,017nm. Power was to be from three RB211-24s developing 45,000lb thrust each, but in May, Rolls-Royce announced a further thrust improvement to 48,000lb. This power bonus would allow the L-1011 to carry 70 more passengers or to increase the maximum range by 400 miles. The gross weight was able to grow to

516,000lb. Lockheed was considering two -2 versions, one offering a range of 4,600nm with 256 passengers and a long-range, shorter fuselage version carrying 216 passengers on long thin routes up to 5,400nm.

In early 1974, the 4,600nm range L-1011-2 was shelved due to the oil supply situation, but in the short term, Lockheed was concentrating on modification of the existing L-1011-1 with an extra fuel tank between the centre-section wing spars and a maximum take-off weight of 466,000lb. In the longer term, the stretched L-1011-3 was being considered increasing the length by anywhere between 20-40ft. Maximum taxi weight was restrained to 525,000lb due to footprint pressure limitations on the existing main undercarriage.

The production launch of the L-1011-200, formerly the '-2', came with the Saudia order on 19 September 1974, powered by three 48,000lb thrust RB211-524 engines. As well as developing the engine for the TriStar, the British Government also backed a 50,000lb thrust version for the Boeing 747. The improvements to the basic L-1011-1 became known as the L-1011-100, the major difference being the engine installation. The '-100' continued to be powered by the RB211-22B or '-22F', while the '-200' was powered by the new RB211/524 engine.

At the end of 1974 Lockheed made presentations to Aeroflot and a number of Western airlines of a new uprated version of the TriStar, known as the L-1011-250. It had an increase in gross weight of 18,000lb over the '-200' to a total of 484,000lb, the extra weight being used for additional fuel tankage to increase the range to 3,500nm. The overall dimensions were unchanged and power would come from three 48,000lb thrust RB211-524 engines.

In the spring of 1975, RB211-524 bench testing was progressing well, with 1,600hr running including a series of 150hr endurance tests. The first engine was expected to fly in the TriStar prototype by the end of the year and full flight testing programmed in a Saudi TriStar in mid-1976. The British Government was funding development of this version of the engine to a value of £26.3 million, recovered by a levy on engine sales. Similar contributions were made for the uprated RB211-524 for the Boeing 747.

By the end of September 1975, Rolls-Royce had delivered the 500th RB211 engine to Lockheed, five years after delivery of the first engine to Palmdale. All but £1 million of the £250 million advanced by the British Government for production funding had been repaid, allowing a profit on production for future deliveries. These profits were then able to offset the £125 million launch costs, which were still to be paid.

In November 1975, Lockheed announced what was to be its major long-range TriStar development, aimed at the 707/DC-8 replacement market of long thin routes, Lockheed specified the L-1011-500 to answer a BA requirement for the early 1980s. The -500 combined the strengthened structure and 50,000lb thrust RB211-524 engines of the '-250', with a fuselage 20ft 2in shorter. Fuel capacity was increased by 22,000lb over the '-250' by extra centre section tankage taking range up to 5,380nm with 231 passengers. Maximum take-off weight could be 490,000lb and at this stage the wing was largely unchanged, apart from thicker skins.

Left:
Like the earlier RB211s, the '-524' was supplied complete with pod including intake and exhaust. *Rolls-Royce*

The -500 did not directly replace the high capacity '-250', but the range of the latter at 4,200nm was a little short of that required for the 707/DC-8 replacement. The reduction in length of the fuselage was balanced out with 180in removed ahead of the wing and 62in behind. The lower deck galley of the standard TriStar was moved up to the main deck to allow more room for cargo under the cabin floor. Although the L-1011-500 could have been ready by 1977, it was felt that it would be too early for the market, due to the overcapacity that was available at the time.

The new 50,000lb thrust RB211-524 engine received its British Certificate of Airworthiness at the end of 1975, the first production engine being built ready for delivery to Lockheed in March 1976 for eventual installation in Saudia's long-range TriStars. This engine was dimensionally the same as the RB211-22, making installation easier and further development to a thrust of 53,000lb was expected. The initial RB211-524 engine deliveries were fitted to Lockheed's test and development prototype TriStar for flight trials in both the wing and tail positions. US certification of the new engine followed in March 1976.

By April 1976, the L-1011-500 had changed slightly as the fuselage shortening was reduced to 13ft 6in and the capacity was increased to 246 passengers, to reduce seat/mile costs. The L-1011-250 had been dropped in favour of the '-500'. The maximum take-off weight had been increased to 496,000lb, 400lb weight being used in strengthening the wing and landing gear. The wing centre section was provided with 54,000lb more fuel capacity, the two tanks feeding the main wing tanks. The range, with the new RB211-524 engines was 5,310nm with a full passenger load. The aircraft would be suitable for such routes as London to Los Angeles, New York to Buenos Aires or Sydney to Hong Kong.

When finally launched by a British Airways order in August 1976, the configuration was 18 first-class and 217 economy-class seats in a fuselage shortened by 100in ahead of the wing and 62in aft.

In the autumn of 1976, Lockheed was investigating other TriStar configurations for future applications. The stretched TriStar 300 would be capable of carrying 410 passengers on the main deck and 45 in a lower deck cabin. This variant was dropped when All-Nippon Airways decided to buy high capacity Boeing 747SRs. By the mid-1980s, Lockheed could see a need for a reduced energy version, the TriStar RE, using extended wingtips, active controls and improved RB211 engines. Later an advanced TriStar could have a new high technology wing. Short- and medium-haul developments could be a '-500'

short fuselage version with the L-1011-1 wing and derated RB211 engines. Studies continued on a twin-engined 200-seater with new wings and tail on the existing fuselage.

In the spring of 1977, Lockheed announced a range of new projects based on the TriStar, and aimed at the medium capacity, short- to medium-range market. The projects still in the conceptual stage were a tri-jet L-1011-400 and the twin-jet L-1011-600. New technology was offered for both versions to provide noise reduction and fuel economy, and included the use of composite materials, improved aerodynamics and active controls. The '-400' was optimised with a maximum take-off weight of between 350,500lb and 374,500lb, seating 200 to 250 passengers depending upon fuselage length. The range would have been 2,700nm covering the US transcontinental routes and the RB211-22B engines were to be derated by 10% to improve economy and overhaul life.

The L-1011-600 was to be powered by a pair of 50,000lb thrust RB211-524B engines mounted on the existing TriStar wing. Seating, depending on fuselage length, was to be for between 174 and 200 passengers, maximum take-off weight up to 297,000lb and range between 2,000nm and 2,700nm.

The L-1011-200 extended range TriStar was granted FAA certification in May 1977 for service with Saudia, at new lower noise levels. By late 1977, Lockheed was reporting successful testing of active ailerons fitted to the company-owned prototype TriStar. Extended wingtips were then installed, increasing aspect ratio and reducing induced drag. The active ailerons eased structural loads on the wings caused by gusts and the increase in span reduced fuel burn by some 3.5%. These modifications were incorporated in the L-1011-500s.

During 1978, Lockheed made strenuous efforts to sell its 200-seat L-1011-400, possible launch customers being Pan Am and Delta, but the competition from the Boeing 767 was very strong. By the autumn of 1978 American Airlines was being courted, in competition with the projected trijet Boeing 777. Alternative power plants were also on option, in particular the Pratt & Whitney JT9D-FJ, developing 50,000lb thrust. However, the hopes of the -400 were dashed when both American and Delta chose the Boeing 767 in November 1978, leaving the long-range '-500' as the major development.

In the latter half of 1979, Lockheed was busy with studies for a TriStar freighter modified to run on liquid hydrogen (LH_2) fuel. The aircraft would be stretched to the limit of its fuselage length and have installed in the fuselage two LH_2 fuel tanks. The forward and rear tanks would have a fuel

capacity of 50,070lb, leaving a cargo capacity in between of 106,330lb. The aircraft was perceived as a long-range freighter on an experimental triangular route service between USA, Europe and the Middle East. It was estimated that the development of hydrogen technology would take two to three years, and a further four years to modify aircraft and construct ground storage facilities for the fuel.

A more conventional freighter was offered to Flying Tiger Line in October 1979, as a modified '-500' with the cabin windows deleted and a new freight door fitted. Maximum payload increased from 97,860lb of the passenger version, to 146,400lb for the cargo carrier, which could be carried over 925nm. Range increased to 3,300nm with a cargo load of 128,400lb. This version was not developed, although conversions were eventually engineered by Marshall of Cambridge for the RAF TriStars.

By September 1980, Lockheed had shelved plans for the L-1011 freighter and was concentrating its future plans on a modern-technology stretched TriStar 500. It was to have the '-200' fuselage with strengthened '-500' wings and active controls. This aircraft would have a transatlantic or transcontinental range. A 'hot and high' TriStar 500 was proposed in the spring of 1981, powered by the Rolls-Royce RB211-524D4 engines developing 53,000lb thrust, an increase of 3,000lb thrust over the existing engines.

Lockheed also developed composite ailerons and fin, the carbon reinforced plastic ailerons being each 65lb lighter than the metal equivalents. The fin, which weighed 630lb, a 27% reduction on the metal equivalent, was the largest composite structure at that time, but was not flown on the aircraft. However, the fin was subjected to static testing to destruction, and a number of components were environmentally tested.

With the cessation of the TriStar programme all major development halted and the original prototype was dismantled to be used for spares. Lockheed has continued to offer modest product improvements to existing operators, mainly aimed at better fuel consumption, greater range, improved reliability and easier maintenance.

As part of this programme, a package was offered in October 1985 by Rolls-Royce and Lockheed, giving the earlier TriStar a long-range capability. This involved re-engining with upgraded RB211-524B4 engines and structural modifications to boost the nominal maximum range from 2,700nm to 4,500nm. The structural strengthening concentrated on key areas of the wing, fuselage and undercarriage, increasing the maximum take-off weight by 15% to 496,000lb and the fuel capacity from 150,560lb to 213,640lb. The modified aircraft became the L-1011-250 and Delta was the first customer for six conversion kits. All TriStars from No 52 onwards were capable of benefiting from these changes apart from the L-1011-500, which already incorporated the improvements. Each conversion required between five and eight weeks to complete at a total investment of $35 million per aircraft including the change of engines. While Lockheed and Rolls-Royce provided the conversion kit, it was expected that the operator would undertake the work on its own premises with the manufacturer's assistance where necessary.

8 British Airways Operations

The TriStar was probably the most significant catalyst for the effective merging of the European and Overseas Divisions of British Airways into one major airline, due to the fact that it was the only aircraft operated by the two divisions.

In 1972 what was then British European Airways (BEA) was looking for a new technology high-capacity wide bodied jet liner for its European and Near East destinations. The three major contenders were the McDonnell Douglas DC-10, the projected British Aircraft Corporation BAC211, which was never to leave the drawing board, and the Lockheed TriStar. The latter became the winner of this order when a contract was signed for nine L-1011-1 TriStars with options on a further six. They could carry between 346 and 398 passengers, or a payload of 29,000kg, on medium range routes up to 3,000nm. Power came from three RB211-22 B engines developing 42,000lb thrust each.

Deliveries commenced with G-BBAE in October 1974, with the first revenue flight two months later to Malaga under the command of Capt Charles Owens.

In 1974 BEA had merged with BOAC and since the nine BEA TriStars were under-utilised, four of the L-1011-1s were operated by the Overseas Division on the Middle Eastern routes.

With the formation of British Airways in 1974, a longer-range version of the TriStar was required, initially designated as the L-1011-250 powered by RB211B4 (improved) engines developing 50,000lbs thrust. It would have been able to carry a payload of 27,000kg up to 5,000nm on the long thin British Airways routes which did not justify the capacity of a Boeing 747. However, the L-1011-500 with a shorter fuselage and longer span wing was chosen and the six earlier options were converted to a firm order, power coming from three RB211-524 BO/2 engines each giving 50,000lb thrust. Meanwhile an Eastern Airlines L-1011-1 N323EA was leased to British Airways from October 1978 for a 20-month period to be used on the European routes.

On 19 April 1979, the first type acceptance flight was made by Capt Terry Lakin of '-500' G-BFCB from Palmdale and on 25 April; the same pilot flew the first production acceptance flight on B-BFCC. The aircraft were delivered by the end of

the month allowing commercial services to commence on 1 May.

On initial operations it was found that the '-500' was not achieving its guaranteed range performance. To overcome the 8-9% shortfall the RB211-524B4 engine was retrofitted, providing the same thrust, but improved fuel consumption, and the wingspan was increased by 9ft giving greater lift, allowing the aircraft to fly from London to Los Angeles with a full load. The increase in span raised the gust loads on the wing main spar and therefore active controls were fitted to reduce these loads and avoid any structural problems. Another problem found was that at high Mach number and high gravity forces the wing tips caused a pitch up resulting in buffet and probable loss of control. This very remote situation was only likely to happen with an aft loaded centre of gravity and precautions were taken on overall operations to keep clear of the critical flight condition until suitable permanent cures could be developed. The American FAA specified a high speed stick shaker to warn of the approach of the critical Mach number, but the British CAA insisted on a rather more costly recovery speed brake to avoid the pitch up.

The L-1011-500 introduced a flight management system (FMS), BA being the launch customer. The FMS gave an area navigation capability using an inertial platform updated by the distance measuring equipment (DME) and (VOR). As well as controlling lateral navigation, it also controlled the climb, cruise and descent to give best fuel economy. Originally this involved much throttle movement of the engines, which Rolls-Royce predicted would dramatically shorten engine life. To overcome this problem and give the engine smooth operation, the TriStar would climb gradually to reduce speed or go into a shallow descent to increase. The change of altitude was only through a matter of 100ft or so and would not be detected by the passengers. The cost of £0.75 million to retrofit the L-1011-1 fleet with FMS was saved every three to four months with the reduction in fuel costs.

All the BA TriStars had a full autoland capability built in from the start. The Collins triple autopilot flared the aircraft at 30ft, but instead of using 'kick-off drift' which could cause the aircraft to

drift too far to one side, one wing was automatically trimmed slightly low to overcome any crosswind component. The TriStar was the first aircraft to be certificated to land in zero visibility and with a zero decision height. Direct lift control uses spoilers to maintain stable approach in pitch. The FMS was introduced on all the BA TriStars and in 1978 the European and Overseas Divisions' TriStars were combined into one fleet. The L-1011-1 aircraft were modified for common crew operation, all aircraft being wired for triple INS, although only one was fitted for short-range operations, the triple installation being reserved for long overwater flights on the '-200' and '-500'. With other changes on the flight deck, common crew operation was introduced, one of the major problems to overcome being the resolution of the relevant crew seniority.

In 1980, there was a need to operate the L-1011-1 to the USA, but it was range limited. However, it was found that the last three aircraft in the batch, G-BEAK to G-BEAM featured additional structural modification, built in on the production line, giving them the designation L-1011-50. All that BA needed to do was change the wheels and axles, literally an overnight job, and the aircraft could carry an additional nine tons of payload, allowing easy operation to the East Coast of the USA. The L-1011-50 is powered by 42,000lb thrust RB211 22B engines giving a range of 3,300nm with a payload of 29,000kg. However, the L-1011-200 are used more regularly to and from New York where their autoland capability is particularly appreciated during the winter months, allowing TriStars to operate into London Airport (LAP) when other aircraft may have to divert to other destinations.

With the amalgamation of the TriStar fleet in BA, further long range high capacity aircraft were required. Orders were placed for eight L-1011-200s with options on four more which in the event were not taken up. The '-200' is a high capacity aircraft powered by three 50,000lb thrust RB211-524 BO/2 engines giving a range of 3,600nm and a payload of up to 31,000kg. This mid-range aircraft could fly to the Middle East or any part of the US East Coast down as far as Miami. Depending upon configuration the '-200' could carry between 250 and 400 passengers. The first acceptance of the '-200' was on G-BGBB on 5 March 1980 by Capt Terry Lakin, which was delivered five days later ready for service entry soon after. The last two '-200s' were leased to British Airtours at Gatwick, the charter subsidiary of BA.

Following the Falklands campaign, the RAF realised that it had an urgent need for long range high capacity tanker/transport aircraft. Although the McDonnell Douglas DC-10 was considered as it had already been re-engineered for this task for the USAF, the ex-BA TriStar 500s were chosen and bought from BA to help the airline with a shortage of cash flow. The six L-1011-500s were withdrawn from service with BA during 1983, the last flight with an airline crew being on 12 December when Capt Terry Lakin flew the aircraft from Boscombe Down on a formation exercise with RAF fighter aircraft to assess the compatibility for flight refuelling. The aircraft were initially delivered to RAF Brize Norton where following crew training, they were used on long range trooping flights, often with BA flight and cabin crew members, pending delivery of the aircraft to Marshall at Cambridge for conversion to tankers. Three more L-1011-500s were later bought from Pan Am.

In early 1985, politics decreed regional route exchanges with British Caledonian, and BA

regretted the disposal of its TriStar 500s. Two were subsequently leased from Air Lanka and reregistered G-BLUS and G-BLUT for the newly acquired South American routes to Bogota, Caracas, Rio and San Paulo. These continued in operation at least until early 1988.

The TriStar-500 and, following their disposal, the '-200s', have been used widely for long range Royal flights. The first one was under command of Capt Terry Lakin in '-500' G-BFCA, carrying HM the Queen to Fiji, leaving Heathrow on 1 November 1982. A year later a TriStar took HM the Queen, to Nairobi via Geneva and Akrotiri, then on to Dakar and Delhi before returning to Heathrow. Other Royal tours in the TriStar have included Amman, Portugal, the Caribbean and Belize, Australia, New Zealand and China. For these flights, the first class cabin was fitted with a special layout including a large centrally placed table with four first-class seats around it, and a couch along the side of the cabin. To the rear is a bedroom and dressing room, and behind that in the business class cabin are located 50 to 60 first-class seats for the Royal household. In the rear cabin, tourist class seats are retained for BA staff and any additional passengers.

British Airways undertakes all major maintenance of the TriStar airframe and engines at Heathrow. They also have been awarded maintenance contracts for the TriStars of Gulf Air, Saudia, the RAF and British Airtours. The maintenance cycle of the TriStar consists of a number of checks. A transit check is completed at every stop and consists of a walkround inspection in case of any damage. A Ramp Check 1 is completed once every calandar day and largely consists of topping up all the consumables such as oil, water, hydraulic fluid and tyre pressures. A Ramp Check 2 is completed not more than 150 flying hours, the Ramp Check 3 up to 300 flying hours and Ramp Check 4 up to 600 flying hours.

Major base maintenance starts with a Service Check 1 to be completed not exceeding 850 flying hours, subject to satisfactory samples being taken at 750hr. A Service Check 2 is up to 1,600 flying hours with samples at 1,300hr and a Service Check 3 is up to 3,100 flying hours. Inter Check 1 is completed up to 4,000 flying hours and Inter Check 2 is up to 8,000 flying hours. These checks cover full structural audit and repairs where necessary of the airframe, replacement of lifed items, overhaul of equipment and incorporation of modifications.

A high utilisation is maintained, the L-1011-1 short haul aircraft achieving 5hr to 6hr a day on up to six round trips from London to Paris, the low hours being as a result of the many turnaround times on the ground. The TriStar -200s average around 10hr per day and the '-500s' achieve between 15hr and 20hr per day.

Normal BA TriStar crewing is with two pilots and a flight engineer, while Airtours sometimes use three pilots. Most of the captains were trained at Hamble, while others are ex-RAF aircrew. Promotion usually comes from captains of narrow bodied jets to the wide-bodied TriStar. Crew training and conversion is completed on a pair of simulators covering the L-1011-1 and L-1011-200. These simulators are also used for refresher flying, instrument rating renewals and any special development flying. A captain and copilot are trained to the same standard, flying 40hr on the simulator and a maximum of 1.5hr on base training covering three circuits. These circuits, often made at Stansted or Prestwick where the air space is not too busy, and the landing charges are lower, usually consist of a normal take off, an engine failure, a two engine

go-around and a landing. This qualifies the crew for a Group 1 endorsement.

Capt Terry Lakin, Flight Manager (Technical) TriStar, has been associated with the BA TriStar operations since they were first ordered by BEA. He is now responsibe for the operation of the TriStar fleet including check lists, drills, modifications, acceptances, certification, certificate of airworthiness air tests and further developments. Capt Lakin was a training captain and can still fly route checks as a type rating examiner and instrument rating examiner, although some of these can be flown on the simulators. Even with all these responsibilities, he has to fly the normal routes 40% of his time.

British Airtours (based at Gatwick) is the charter subsidiary of BA which started with ex-BEA Comet 4Bs and ex-BOAC Boeing 707s. It now dry leases on average three TriStar-1s and the three TriStar -50s from the BA main line fleet, although the fleet size depends upon seasonal demand. In addition to operating charters in its own right Airtours also operates the BA mainline services from Gatwick to Malta and Spain on wet lease back to the parent organisation. With the takeover of British Caledonian Airways, the TriStars are now operated in the colours of Caledonian Airways, the new charter division of British Airways.

Although it is planned to replace the short to medium range TriStars with Boeing 767s in a year or two, and the long thin '-500' routes with either Airbus A340 or McDonnell Douglas MD-11, the TriStar is still a very effective and adaptable aircraft. Its advanced technology has kept it up to date, and it will be difficult to replace directly in the near future. The low noise levels of the engines give exemption from the night jet ban at Heathrow and at some airfields the landing fees are reduced, penalising the noisier jets. The TriStar has therefore been, and continues to be, an asset to British Airways.

9 Marshall: Support and Conversion

Marshall of Cambridge is unique in the modern aerospace industry in being a family business, founded in 1909 and still managed by Sir Arthur Marshall, chairman and managing director, who is the son of the founder. Now in his 80s, Sir Arthur still maintains an active interest in the business, working a full day and communicating closely with his staff, many of whom have built up long years of service with the Company.

Cambridge Airport has had a long association with Lockheed through its work on the support of the Hercules military freighter, but this association expanded with work on the TriStars, although there is no formal agreement between the companies.

It was the Falklands campaign which created the need within the RAF for additional tanker/transport capacity. Prior to this campaign the Victor tankers of Nos 55 and 57 Squadrons had

been expected to serve well into the 1990s to be replaced by the VC10 tankers followed by a new as yet to be specified design. However, not only did the Falklands campaign underline the importance of long range air-to-air refuelling, it also used up prematurely the fatigue life on the Victor K2 tankers. A replacement was therefore required urgently, not only as an aerial tanker, but a long range transport to support the military garrison in the Falklands.

In the second half of 1982, when the requirement was being established, there were a number

Below:
Typical underfloor fuel tanks ready for installation in the RAF TriStar tankers.
Marshall of Cambridge (Engineering) Ltd

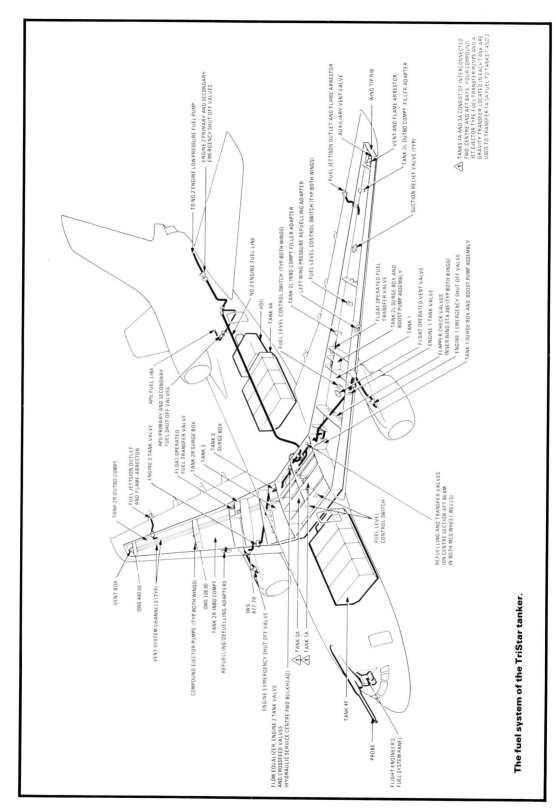

The fuel system of the TriStar tanker.

TO NO 2 ENGINE LOW PRESSURE FUEL PUMP

ENGINE 2 PRIMARY AND SECONDARY
EMERGENCY SHUT OFF VALVES

FUEL JETTISON OUTLET AND FLAME ARRESTOR

AUXILIARY VENT VALVE

WING TIP RIB

VENT AND FLAME ARRESTOR

TANK 2L OUTBD COMPT FILLER ADAPTER

SUCTION RELIEF VALVE (TYP)

NO 2 ENGINE FUEL LINE

FUEL LEVEL CONTROL SWITCH (TYP BOTH WINGS)

TANK 2L INBD COMPT FILLER ADAPTER

LEFT WING PRESSURE REFUELLING ADAPTER

FUEL LEVEL CONTROL SWITCH (TYP BOTH WINGS)

HDU

TANK 4A

FLOAT OPERATED FUEL
TRANSFER VALVE

TANK 2L SURGE BOX AND
BOOST PUMP ASSEMBLY

TANK 1

FLOAT OPERATED VENT VALVE

ENGINE 1 TANK VALVE

FLAPPER CHECK VALVES
INSR WING STA 346 (TYP BOTH WINGS)

ENGINE 1 EMERGENCY SHUT OFF VALVE

TANK 1 SURGE BOX AND BOOST PUMP ASSEMBLY

APU FUEL LINE

APU PRIMARY AND SECONDARY
FUEL SHUT OFF VALVES

FLOAT OPERATED
FUEL TRANSFER VALVE

TANK 2R SURGE BOX

TANK 3

TANK 3
SURGE BOX

ENGINE 3 TANK VALVE

FUEL JETTISON OUTLET
AND FLAME ARRESTOR

TANK 2R OUTBD COMPT

VENT BOX

OWS 440.50

VENT SYSTEM CHANNELS (TYP)

COMPOUND EJECTOR PUMPS (TYP BOTH WINGS)

OWS 126.80

TANK 2R INBD COMPT

REFUELLING/DEFUELLING ADAPTERS

IWS
477.70

ENGINE 3 EMERGENCY SHUT OFF VALVE

TANK 3A

TANK 1A

FLOW EQUALIZER, ENGINE 2 TANK VALVE
AND CROSSFEED VALVES
(HYDRAULIC SERVICE CENTRE FWD BULKHEAD)

TANK 4F

PROBE

FLIGHT ENGINEER'S
FUEL SYSTEM PANEL

FUEL LEVEL
CONTROL SWITCH

REFUELLING AND TRANSFER VALVES
(ON CENTRE SECTION AFT BEAM
IN BOTH MLG WHEEL WELLS)

⚠ TANKS 1A AND 3A CONSIST OF INTERCONNECTED
FWD, CENTRE AND AFT BAYS. FOUR COMPOUND
JET EJECTOR TYPE FUEL TRANSFER PUMPS AND A
GRAVITY TRANSFER LOCATED IN EACH TANK ARE
USED TO TRANSFER 1A-3A FUEL TO TANKS 1 AND 3

74

of commercial jet transports on the market, making a conversion task the most cost effective solution. The choice was between the six TriStar 500s with British Airways or the ex-Laker DC-10s. The competing proposals were made by Marshall in association with Lockheed for the TriStar conversion, and McDonnell Douglas with British Aerospace and possibly British Caledonian.

Following a detailed evaluation, the TriStar emerged as the final choice, since despite the availability of the KC-10A tanker derivative of the DC-10, there was little advantage in the conversion of a civil airliner. The decision to purchase the six BA TriStar 500s was announced on 14 December 1982 and the conversion contract was awarded to Marshall in February 1983. Marshall then became the UK design authority for the tanker/freighter conversion of the Lockheed TriStar for the RAF and rapidly constructed a new hangar, capable of accommodating five TriStars in work at any one time. During 1984, three more TriStar 500s were acquired from Pan Am, to a generally similar standard to the BA aircraft. The acquisition of the TriStar gave the RAF a tanker/transport capability which it had not had previously.

The conversion and introduction into service of the TriStars has been in a number of phases, two of the three ex-Pan Am TriStars entering service purely as passenger transports, leaving the third aircraft stored at Cambridge. Meanwhile, the BA aircraft were converted in three phases. The first four emerged initially as K1 tanker/passenger aircraft, the first conversion making its maiden flight from Cambridge on 9 July 1985, the second conversion being the first to enter service with No 216 Squadron at Brize Norton. The first two aircraft were delivered to an interim standard, while number three and four were to full K1 standard. The fifth and sixth aircraft were to the revised K1 tanker/freighter standard incorporating a forward upper deck freight door, a cargo handling system with reinforcement where required. The first two aircraft are the next K1 conversions, followed by the remaining pair of aircraft. The three ex-Pan Am aircraft differ in detail, which makes it impossible to modify them to the identical standard of the ex-BA aircraft.

They will therefore be designated K2 as tanker-passenger transports. All nine aircraft will later be capable of having flight refuelling Mk 32 refuelling pods under each wing, making them capable of flight refuelling a pair of combat aircraft simultaneously.

The modification of the ex-BA TriStars to tanker configuration involves the installation, with local reinforcing where required, of extra fuel tanks in the main underfloor forward C1 and rear C2 cargo compartments, and twin flight refuelling Mk 17T hose-drogue drum units (HDU) in the aft end C3 cargo compartment. The C3 entry, which allows access to the HDUs without removal of the rear fuel tanks, is not present on the ex-Pan Am TriStars, reducing the available underfloor tankage accordingly. The fuel tanks themselves are very much like double size heavy duty underfloor containers, which are installed through the existing cargo doors and plumbed together. The forward C1 freight compartment holds four fuel tanks with a pump/collector box, while the rear C2 compartment holds three tanks and a pump/collector box, increasing the TriStar fuel capacity by up to a maximum of 100,000lb. The TriStars can also receive fuel, due to the installation of a probe attached to the upper surface of the forward fuselage above the cockpit roof. It is slightly offset to starboard to allow easier visual reference by the captain and is set with a negative incidence of 7° to compensate for the normal nose up incidence of the TriStar in flight.

The twin HDUs are installed, so that each one is capable of independent operation to ensure that no single failure will cause an air to air mission to be aborted. The HDUs are installed side by side in a pressure box, allowing the aircraft to carry out air to air refuelling operations while maintaining normal cabin pressure. The conversion provides for the transfer of fuel from either HDU at a rate compatible with a receiver aircraft, up to

Top right:
The installation of the main deck freight door on the TriStar includes a large reinforced area to maintain the structural integrity.
Marshall of Cambridge (Engineering) Ltd

Below right:
The TriStar fuselage is very carefully de-stressed and supported for the installation of the large freight door cut-out.
Marshall of Cambridge (Engineering) Ltd

Below:
TriStar KMk 1 ZD951 after conversion to tanker by Marshall at Cambridge.
Marshall of Cambridge (Engineering) Ltd

Above:
Following the freight door structural installation, the up and over door is fitted.
Marshall of Cambridge (Engineering) Ltd

500gal/min over a speed range of 180kt to 320kt at altitudes of up to 35,000ft.

By the end of 1987, three of the K1 aircraft were in service with the RAF, while ZD950 was in use with Marshall on a flight development pro-gramme to clear hose drum modifications and the new avionics fit. During the first six months of 1988, this development aircraft was operated on CA clearance trials at Boscombe Down, allowing air-to-air refuelling capability to be proved with all anticipated receiver aircraft. Meanwhile in the Marshall hangar, the first two conversions were being made to the full cargo configuration on ZD948 and ZD952.

The C4 cargo door installation consists of an upper deck upward-opening freight door measuring 140in by 102in on the port side of the forward cabin. To achieve such a large cutout in the fuselage, the entire aircraft had to be carefully supported and jacked to remove all stresses and loads from the structure, otherwise major

distortion would have occurred. The actual installation involved cut out and reinforcing around the aperture of double the area of the door to cope with the structural loads. The cabin floor was reinforced to allow the carriage of 16,000lb pallets, and power rollers and winches were installed to move heavy loads. The tanker/freighter variants are capable of carrying up to 100,000lb freight, or can be rapidly role changed to a 200-troop carrier or troop/freight mixed configuration, depending upon the type of pallets fitted in the fuselage. The first conversion with the C4 cargo door, ZD948 was subjected to a structural test programme in the new TriStar hangar, simulating a 2.5g turning load with the aircraft pressurised, to represent the worst flight condition. During this structural test the aircraft was fully instrumented to measure the relevant loads.

In addition to its work on TriStars for the RAF, Marshall also received a contract from British Airways to complete the Sunset III conversions on the long fuselage TriStars. This work on the longer range L-1011-50s and L-1011-200s involved 10 aircraft and basically consisted of removing the below main deck floor galleys to the upper deck to increase the capacity of the C1 cargo bay, and to reconfigure and refurbish the passenger cabins. This work was completed to a

Lockheed service bulletin and did not involve Marshall in any design work, the first aircraft to be completed being G-BHBR.

Although the TriStar is still a very advanced aircraft in terms of its systems, newer aircraft are now becoming available which will replace the fleets in service with the initial operators. This will put on the market a number of modern highly economical wide-bodied jets still with an adequate fatigue life to keep them commercially viable for many years to come.

Marshall is, therefore, in close communications with the current airliner manufacturers, which might well be taking TriStars in part exchange for their new products, to offer a cost-effective freighter conversion capability to the existing airframes. Conversion to freighter or freighter/passenger (combi) can be made to any existing airframes by fitting the C4 upper deck cargo door on the port side using the experience gained with the conversion of the RAF aircraft. The freighter conversion programme is fully supported by the Lockheed Aeronautical Systems Company, for-merly the Lockheed California Company. The main deck can be reinforced depending upon the operators requirements, and the total maximum load in the main cabin is 23 88in by 125in pallets. In addition 16 LD-3 containers up to a weight of 36,000lb can be carried in the forward cargo hold, and eight more up to 18,000lb in the rear cargo hold. A typical single class combi layout could have seating for up to 202 passengers, a cargo load on the main deck of 58,400lb in eight cargo pallets and below floor cargo capacity of up to 63,750lb.

Marshall of Cambridge therefore have an ongoing association with the TriStar, both with the RAF and in planned future business as fleets of the aircraft appear on the secondhand market.

Below:
Once the new large freight door was fitted to the TriStar by Marshall, non-destructive testing was undertaken to proof test the worst case loading.
Marshall of Cambridge (Engineering) Ltd

Maximum main deck pallet installation — freighter configuration.

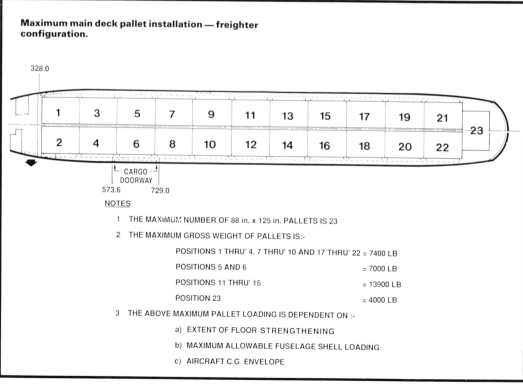

NOTES

1   THE MAXIMUM NUMBER OF 88 in. x 125 in. PALLETS IS 23

2   THE MAXIMUM GROSS WEIGHT OF PALLETS IS:-

        POSITIONS 1 THRU' 4, 7 THRU' 10 AND 17 THRU' 22 = 7400 LB

        POSITIONS 5 AND 6   = 7000 LB

        POSITIONS 11 THRU' 16   = 13900 LB

        POSITION 23   = 4000 LB

3   THE ABOVE MAXIMUM PALLET LOADING IS DEPENDENT ON :-

        a) EXTENT OF FLOOR STRENGTHENING

        b) MAXIMUM ALLOWABLE FUSELAGE SHELL LOADING

        c) AIRCRAFT C.G. ENVELOPE

10 Safety

The modern airliner with its high technology computer-based systems is inherently a safer vehicle of transportation than its predecessors. The automatic flight systems provide a consistency of operation which is largely monitored by the crew, and avoids wherever possible the variations caused by human error. The Lockheed TriStar was an advanced aircraft for its time, a sophistication which cost the manufacturer a great deal in development, but has brought very real advantages to the operators and passengers in terms of reliability and safety. In such a complex product as a jet airliner, systems can still fail, but should have the safeguards to fail soft, and not a catastrophic fail hard.

The first of the wide-bodied jets to be lost in an accident was Lockheed TriStar N310EA which had been delivered to Eastern Airlines on 18 August 1972. The aircraft was allocated to operate Eastern Flight 401 from New York to Miami on 29 December 1972 with a load of 163 passengers and 13 crew members. On approach to Miami, the nosewheel locked-down indication light on the pilots' instrument panels failed to illuminate. As a precaution, the TriStar overshot the airport and climbed to 2,000ft to the west to investigate the malfunction. In trying to replace the undercarriage indicator light, one of the pilots inadvertently knocked the control column, which unknown to the crew could disengage the autopilot. While the captain was busy trying to change the light bulb, the first officer was monitoring the flying of the aircraft on the autopilot, which according to his instrumentation

Left:
The Marshall hangar at Cambridge can accommodate up to five TriStars in work at any one time.
Marshall of Cambridge (Engineering) Ltd

Below:
The wreckage of Eastern Airlines TriStar N310EA was widely scattered by its impact in the Everglades swamps near Miami. Surprisingly 76 of the occupants survived this accident. *Associated Press*

was still switched on. The second officer, in effect, the flight engineer, meanwhile climbed down through a hatch in the cockpit floor to the 'hell hole' to check the lock down of the nose wheel through a special telescope.

During this time, with the crew unaware, the aircraft was in a gradual descent over the Everglade Swamps in Florida, the loss of height remaining undetected due to the darkness outside, close to midnight, with no external visual references. Neither pilot could see the other's instrument panel. The TriStar hit the swamp in a level attitude 17 miles west of Miami International Airport, breaking up on impact and although the crash was classed as nonsurvivable, the resilient structure of the TriStar resulted in 76 out of the 176 persons on board surviving. Amongst the survivors of the crash impact were some of the flight deck crew members. Capt Bob Loft was still alive when the first rescuers arrived at the scene, but died before medical care was available. The First Officer, Bert Stockstill was killed on impact. Down in the 'hell hole' under the cockpit floor, both Don Repo, the Second Officer, and Angelo Donadeo, an Eastern Airlines technical trouble shooter, who had been riding in the cockpit jump seat, were still alive, but badly injured. Don Repo later died in hospital of his injuries. Angelo Donadeo recovered and was able to help the investigators with details of the cockpit activities up to the time he went into the 'hell hole' to assist Don Repo, to identify the undercarriage problem.

The flight-data recorder and the cockpit voice recorder were recovered, the former indicating the rate of descent for 3min prior to impact. The cockpit voice recorder had confirmed the single chime had sounded to indicate the aircraft had left its assigned altitude, but this sounded on the flight engineer's panel, while he was under the floor and the two pilots were too busy with the light indicator to hear the warning above the noise in the cockpit.

The subsequent report issued by the US National Transportation Safety Board following a public enquiry attributed the prime cause of the accident to the failure of the flight crew to monitor the flight instruments during the last four minutes of the flight. It was stated that none of the aircraft systems was a contributory factor to the accident. However, if a $12.00 indicator system had not failed and the autopilot had not been so easy to disengage, the crew would not have been placed in such a disastrous situation. The nosewheel was subsequently found to have been locked down.

There was a mysterious sequel to the crash of Flight 401, well documented in a book called *The Ghost of Flight 401*, by John G. Fuller. Despite the force of impact of the Eastern TriStar in the Everglades swamp, some sections of the aircraft remained as major pieces and contained virtually undamaged black boxes and galley equipment. After the accident investigation, much of this serviceable equipment was salvaged and installed later in Eastern TriStar N318EA, as well as other aircraft in the fleet.

During a flight on N318EA several months after the accident, one of the flight attendants saw the face of the Flight 401 flight engineer, Don Repo, looking out at her from one of the ovens. A second stewardess went down to the galley confirming the apparition. The flight engineer was called down and not only did he see the vision, but it communicated. He was warned of a future fire on the aircraft by Don Repo.

Shortly after, the aircraft was in Mexico City, when a problem developed with one of its engines. Permission was given for a two engine ferry flight without passengers to the maintenance base for an engine change. However, soon after take-off a fire developed in one of the remaining engines causing it to be shut down. With great skill, and maybe some help from the supernatural, the crew brought the aircraft round and landed safely on one engine, never having gone any higher than 400ft above ground level.

On another occasion, TriStar N318EA was on a turnaround at Newark for a departure to Miami. While the flight deck crew were running through their preflight cockpit checks, the cabin staff were making a routine headcount of passengers. In the first-class section, the senior stewardess appeared to have one extra passenger. The unaccounted passenger was an Eastern Airlines Captain in uniform, which was not uncommon, as the captains often returned in spare seats in first-class, later probably moving to the jump seat on the flight deck. When the stewardess questioned the captain's plans she received no response despite a repeated request. The flight supervisor was no more successful, so the aircraft captain was called. The regular passengers in the area of the first-class cabin were anxious about what was going on, and the captain approached the seat to clear up the problem. He was puzzled as there was no record of another Eastern Captain travelling on his flight. With both the stewardess and flight supervisor, the flight captain leaned across to address the other captain. He suddenly froze and said, 'My God, it's Bob Loft'. The rest of the cabin was silent, and all of a sudden, the mystery figure vanished. Despite a thorough search of the aircraft, the missing captain could not be found.

There were other occasions when both dead crew members appeared on N318EA, and some other Eastern TriStars, Don Repo being the most frequent. There were no reports of the reappearance of First Officer Stockstill. Obtaining evidence through eyewitnesses was made difficult due to the Eastern Airlines' policy of sending anyone reporting these sightings to the company psychiatrist, the individual possibly being later grounded or laid off.

The second major incident which befell a TriStar was on 19 April 1974, with TWA TriStar N31007 which was parked unattended and locked up for the night at Boston Logan Airport when a fire broke out in the rear fuselage. Although parts of the aircraft were salvageable, it was unrepairable and declared a total loss on the insurance. The fire was believed to have started near the APU, but the subsequent investigation cleared the engines and APU from being in any way the cause of the destruction of the aircraft, although the reason for the start of the fire was never determined. There were no injuries in this incident.

Following the loss of the Turkish DC-10 near Paris due to the inflight opening of an underfloor cargo door, all wide-bodied aircraft were required to be fitted with cabin floor venting, to avoid the pressurisation collapsing the floor and jamming the controls. The TriStar was included in this programme, requiring over 70 changes to the cabin floor even though it was already designed with inward opening plug doors. Once each aircraft was prepared, the modifications took some 1,857 man hours to complete, at a unit cost of $85,000.

A most disturbing and mysterious accident occurred to Saudia TriStar HZ-AHK on 19 August 1980. The aircraft was carrying Moslem pilgrims from Karachi to Mecca, and had landed at Riyadh, before leaving for Jeddah. A fire was discovered in the rear cabin soon after take-off and the captain turned back from 79 miles out to return to Riyadh, but did not apparently declare an emergency, although he reported smoke in the cabin, and at 40 miles out a fire in the cabin. Original speculation had attributed the start of the fire to butane gas stoves carried by some of the passengers, but the seat of the fire was found to have been in the C3 rearward cargo compartment, under the cabin floor, ahead of the rear pressure dome. On the approach, the high intensity of the fire melted the throttle controls to the tail-mounted No 2 engine, which was shut down as it was no longer under control.

On landing, the aircraft cleared the runway and commenced taxying, the captain requesting coaches to transport the passengers, as he intended to order an emergency evacuation. The aircraft came to a halt with the underwing engines continuing to run and the rescue services were unable to open the cabin doors, possibly due to the fact that there was still some residual

Below:
The badly burned remains of Saudia TriStar HZ-AHK at Riyadh on 19 August 1980 when all 301 occupants were killed. *Associated Press*

pressure in the aircraft. The engines were shut down some 6min after landing and it was a further 5min before the No 2 starboard door was opened. By then, there was no sign of life in the cabin and shortly after the entire interior burst into flames, burning through the roof. All 301 people on board died in this accident, which appeared survivable for many on the aircraft, if only escape procedures had been followed promptly. Preliminary investigations had ruled out the engines, APU and fuel systems as sources of the fire, and the fuel tanks did not ignite at any stage.

The captain was criticised for a number of decisions which resulted in the TriStar disaster, one of which was to waste 5min after the fire alarm had sounded, heading away from Riyadh, while the crew investigated the source of the fire. He also wasted time clearing the runway after landing and failed to shut down the wing-mounted engines, resulting in the residual pressurisation, making the doors impossible to open. An eye witness report also suggested that the TriStar did come to a halt on the runway and may have shut down the outboard engines, before restarting them to back track and clear the runway at the nearest turning point. The report of the 180° turn and backtrack was confirmed, but not the engine shutdown and restart. Air traffic had apparently ordered the aircraft to clear the runway although fire vehicles were in attendance, probably as a precaution as no full emergency had been declared, despite passengers dying on board due to the fire and fumes. The captain had asked the fire crew to check for any signs of external fire.

From subsequent analysis of the cockpit voice recorder, a possible sequence of events was built up which still leaves the disturbing fact that for some unknown reason, the captain never declared a full emergency. Seven minutes after take-off a smoke detector aural warning alerted the crew to a problem, but they referred to the wrong section of the checklist. Three minutes after the warning, the American flight engineer went into the cabin to investigate. Seven minutes later a voice is heard to call 'Fire!' but the flight engineer reports 'just smoke' aft. At this point, the captain decides to turn back, and rather than declare an emergency, he appears to sing in Arabic and when the centre engine became difficult to control, he closed it down.

At 18min after the start of the emergency, a voice called 'Fire in the cabin!' and a female cabin attendant was unable to go to the rear due to panic-stricken people in the aisles. Passengers were obviously being overcome with the fumes. While the landing checklist was being called, the captain said, 'No', to turning off the fuel valves, and made no comment about evacuation, continuing to sing in Arabic. After touch down the flight engineer requested the order to evacuate, but the captain made no decision, turned the aircraft off the runway and stopped on the taxiway. There was still no sign externally of a fire. Air traffic was told to 'stand by' when asked if assistance was required, and soon after white smoke was seen under the aircraft, normally associated with burning Skydrol hydraulic fluid. A fire truck requested that the engines be shut off and the last call from the aircraft came 4min after touch down which was, 'We are trying to evacuate now'. There was still no external sign of fire or any Mayday call.

When eventually a door was opened 15min after landing, bodies were found stacked around the exits, and after the resultant fire was extinguished, the flight deck crew were found strapped in their seats. A member of the cabin crew was across the throttle box, buried under a pile of passengers who had burst through the crew door. Although the cause of the fire was never determined for certain, it was suspected that there was a Skydrol leak in the rear equipment bay, which may have rotted adjacent electrical insulation, causing an arc which ignited the flammable fluid. The fire would have released toxic gas, killing everyone on board, before the main fire when the doors were opened.

A further incident happened on 23 December 1980 with a Saudia TriStar, when the port main landing gear tyres exploded at 29,000ft, which drove a wheel rim inward through the fuselage undercarriage bay and blew off the undercarriage door. The explosion, on a Dhahran-Karachi flight, blasted a 5ft by 3ft hole in the fuselage and cabin floor, the resulting decompression sucking two children out of the aircraft. The captain made an emergency descent to Doha, Qatar, with no further incident. Out of the total of 290 passengers and 16 crew, three other passengers received treatment for minor injuries.

On 27 May 1985, British Airtours TriStar G-BBAI overran the runway on landing at Leeds/Bradford Airport after a flight from Majorca. All the 416 passengers were rapidly evacuated, the TriStar suffering serious undercarriage damage, and the 160-tonne aircraft was recovered for repair within 48hr of the incident. The major recommendations to be made following the investigation of this incident was to improve the drainage of wet runways and to investigate landing performance on runways with a significant initial downslope.

On 2 August 1985, Delta Air Lines Flight 191, TriStar N726DA was on approach to Dallas-Fort Worth Airport where a small but severe thunderstorm, known as a microburst, had developed close to the runway threshold. A microburst is a sudden, highly localised downward gust of cold air from the heart of a convective cloud. An aircraft flying into one at low altitude usually encounters a headwind giving an increase in lift, then a violent down draught, and finally a tailwind which produces a sharp loss of airspeed and lift, all in a very short time. This vicious sequence of sudden wind shifts can be powerful enough to force the aircraft into the ground, despite all the pilot's recovery actions.

The crew of the Delta TriStar had not been warned of the severity of the storm on the end of the runway, mainly because the danger had not been appreciated by air traffic control as there was little evidence to cause concern. The TriStar flew into the storm and encountered airspeed fluctuations of plus 20kt to minus 44kt from its normal approach speed with downdrafts of up to 40ft/sec during a period of 32sec. Then in a second, indicated airspeed reduced from 140kt to 120kt, the 40ft/sec downdraft changed to a 20ft/sec updraft and a strong lateral gust hit the aircraft rolling it to the right. The angle of attack increased from 6° to at least 23° and power was increased, but did not stop the aircraft hitting the ground in a ploughed field 6,336ft from the runway threshold, in a wings-level nose-high altitude. The aircraft became airborne for a short while before touching down again just prior to crossing a main road knocking over lamp standards and destroying a car. At this point the aircraft began to shed parts and the collision with the vehicle caused a fire to start in the left side of the cabin. The aircraft headed across rough ground towards water tanks, losing the No 1 engine after hitting a crater, and portions of the nose undercarriage, left tailplane and pieces of the wing control surfaces. The first water tank was grazed, but the TriStar hit the second water tank, after running 3,195ft from initial touchdown,

and broke apart destroying the front fuselage and breaking off the wings.

The aircraft was severely damaged by the impact and resulting post crash fire, 135 of the 163 persons on board being killed. The 28 survivors, including three cabin crew were all in the mid-cabin and rear portion, the latter remaining intact when the front of the aircraft broke away and burst into flames.

During approach to the airport, air traffic control advised the TriStar crew to reduce speed from 210kt, eventually down to 150kt to give adequate separation from a Learjet ahead. On the final approach, Air Traffic advised the TriStar 'go around, do not land', but the pilot may not have received the message. There was no evidence of any failure in aircraft structure, systems or power plant. As a result of this accident, many more wind sheer sensors were installed at a number of airports, although wind sheer and microburst detection would eventually be better detected by Doppler weather radar.

A further rear fuselage underfloor fire occurred on a Royal Jordanian TriStar, JY-AGE, on 18 October 1985, causing cabin depressurisation, followed by an emergency landing at Singapore. On investigation, it was revealed that an electrical cable from No 2 engine generator showed signs of fraying and arcing. The probable reason for the fire was the rubbing of the wires on the air duct, which burned an 8in hole in the aft pressure bulkhead. The captain had been alerted by an

Below:
The majority of the survivors from Delta TriStar N726DA after its crash at Dallas-Fort Worth on 2 August 1985 were seated in the rear cabin which survived the intial impact relatively intact.
Associated Press

overheat warning in the fuselage close to the No 2 centre engine while descending through 20,000ft, followed by an engine fire warning which was subsequently shut down. The cabin depressurised and filled with smoke before landing. Considerable damage was caused to the underfloor area of the fuselage aft of the bleed air duct and to the captain's stabiliser control linkage. Two of the four hydraulic systems were also damaged. There were no casualties in this incident.

The final loss at the time of writing was Air Lanka TriStar 4R-ULD which was written off at Colombo on the ground as a result of sabotage on 3 May 1986. The departure of the aircraft had been delayed when a bomb, packed in a toolkit, exploded, killing 16 passengers and injuring a further 41. The tail end of the aircraft was blown off.

An incident which occurred to a Delta Air Lines TriStar on 13 November 1986 underlined the failsafe characteristics of the aircraft structure. On the approach to land at Newark, New Jersey, an alert air traffic controller reported smoke issuing from the right main undercarriage. This 'smoke' was found to be fuel vapour leaking from a large fracture in the wing-rear spar. The engines were shut down and the passengers and crew evacuated without injury. On examination, it was found that there was a complete separation of the

rear spar between the wing root and landing gear attachment. A 6.75in fatigue crack had reached a critical length during the latter portion of the flight, propogating rapidly through the spar. This TriStar had flown 37,445hr in 21,788 sorties, but subsequent inspection of all TriStars with over 10,000 flight cycles showed no sign of further fatigue cracking.

In a 1982 issue of *Frequent Flyer* magazine, the TriStar was termed 'one of the cleanest, quietest, most technologically advanced aircraft ever produced. It is also one of the safest aircraft flying today.' *Flight International*, well known for its air safety reporting concluded in a study of airliner accident/incident data in January 1983 that 'the best American widebody is the Lockheed TriStar', and also, 'the Lockheed TriStar's popular reputation as a very safe aircraft is endorsed by the record'.

Below:
The complete tail section and rear cabin was blown off Air Lanka TriStar 4R-ULD at Colombo on 3 May 1986. This sabotage act resulted in the death of 16 passengers and injuries to a further 41 when a bomb blew up as the aircraft was being made ready for departure. Departure had been delayed, otherwise no doubt all occupants would have been killed had the aircraft been airborne. *Associated Press*

11 TriStars with the RAF

The RAF operator of the TriStar is No 216 Squadron, pronounced 'two-sixteen', in recognition of its RNAS origins. No 216 Squadron, which celebrated its 70th anniversary in May 1988, has become well known as a transport squadron in recent years, apart from a short spell with Buccaneers, but despite the outward appearance of returning to the transport role, again with the TriStars, it is more of a multi-role unit in a constantly changing environment. At the time of writing, the squadron operates two basic types of TriStar 500s, with some differences in equipment standard in the flight refuelling tanker version, due to the continuing trials and proving programme.

Following the Falklands conflict, the need for a long range strategic flight refuelling tanker aircraft was realised. The structural life of the Victor tankers was limited, especially after the heavy usage during the Falklands campaign, the last of the interim Vulcan tankers were retired, and the Hercules tankers lacked the long range and high performance. This left the newly converted VC10 and Super VC10 tankers to shoulder an ever increasing load and commitment to the NATO needs.

While all the previous aircraft have been dedicated tankers, a long range wide bodied jet could have its underfloor holds filled with extra fuel tanks, and still have room for up to 200 troops and their equipment on the main deck. Both the McDonnell Douglas DC-10 and the Lockheed TriStar were evaluated for the RAF requirements, and despite the existing operation by the USAF of the DC-10 Extenders for flight refuelling, the TriStar proved to be the most cost effective and operationally desirable answer to the requirements. The Extenders bought new from the production line would not only have been expensive, but would have needed modification to the probe and drogue system used by the RAF, rather than the boom system used by the USAF. Secondhand DC-10s would equally have needed major re-engineering.

The availability of the six British Airways TriStar 500s at an affordable price, provided the RAF not only with an effective tanker conversion, but also a wide bodied long range transport capable of resupply of the Falklands or any other long distance destination, at short notice. While Marshall Engineering started the conversion of four of the TriStars to flight refuelling tankers, the remaining two aircraft were allocated to training and transport duties as the first RAF wide-bodied jets.

On 15 August 1983, the first aircrew arrived at RAF Brize Norton to form the nucleus of what was to become No 216 Squadron. The initial commanding officer was Wg Cdr K. D. Filbey.

During the early training period, the squadron personnel flew under the supervision of British Airways flight deck crews, but by February 1984, the RAF crews were fully qualified and continued operating the aircraft in the transport role until June 1985, when these two aircraft were also delivered to Cambridge for conversion to tankers.

Meanwhile in early 1985, a further three TriStar 500s were purchased from Pan Am and in September of the same year two of these aircraft entered service with No 216 Squadron in the air transport role, carrying up to 260 passengers, their major route being a thrice weekly schedule to the Falklands. This has now reduced to twice a week with an additional schedule to Cyprus and other ad hoc long range services. The Pan Am TriStars are, as is to be expected, to a different equipment standard to the ex-BA aircraft, and the third of the Pan Am trio has been in open storage at Cambridge for about three years with its engines and much equipment removed. This aircraft is now likely to enter its refurbishment programme with Marshall Engineering in mid-1988 to become the first of the three-point flight refuelling tankers, with a pair of hose and drogue systems in underwing pods, one on either side. Following the successful conversion of this aircraft, the other two ex-Pan Am aircraft are likely to be converted to the same standard, probably to be designated the KMk 2. This version will then be capable of flight refuelling two aircraft at once, unlike the K1 which can only cope with one aircraft.

In March 1986, the first of the initial six converted K1 tankers was delivered to allow flight training of the crews to commence, although flight refuelling training had to await the clearance by the Aeroplane and Armament Experimental Establishment (A&AEE) at Boscombe Down of the various types of aircraft compatibility with the TriStar. By mid-1988, the Tornado F2 and F3, the Phantoms, VC10s and Victors had been cleared as receivers of fuel from the TriStar, with more to follow. Although the TriStar itself has been fitted with a refuelling probe above the flight deck, in practice, it has been found that it is unlikely, if ever, to be used as

not only does the aircraft carry more than enough fuel for its requirements, but the large fan engines do not respond well to the varying throttle movements required to maintain formation with a tanker aircraft. It is likely therefore that the probes may be removed.

The TriStar K1 carries 200 passengers in forward facing seats, a break with RAF tradition, all to the rear of the original central galley. In the forward area are roller mats allowing the storage of baggage containers which are loaded through the forward access door. Larger pallets will be capable of loading when the new freight door is fitted. There are galleys fore and aft, the rear ones mainly to serve the passengers while the forward galley provides the crew with refreshments, behind which is a crew rest area for very long flights.

Additional equipment on the flight deck includes Tacan, two UHF (Ultra High Frequency) radio sets, IFF (Identification Friend or Foe), Omega navigation aid and a radio relay for Search and Rescue assistance. Normal equipment retained from commercial service includes a VOR (VHF Omni Range), DME, two ADF (Automatic Direction Finders), and three INS and the FMS. Autoland is still fitted, although not used operationally by the RAF, but the twin autopilot is used fully.

Above:
The TriStar K1 has 200 passenger seats in the rear cabin and space for baggage containers at the forward end. *P. J. Birtles*

Right:
The TriStar KMk 1 has twin HDUs, only one of which is used at a time. The video camera is in the underfuselage dome just forward of the HDUs, allowing visual monitoring of the flight refuelling. *P. J. Birtles*

The training for the RAF TriStar fleet is started with a 17-day ground school course with British Airways followed by 11 4hr sessions on the BA TriStar simulator. The crews then report to No 216 Squadron for two base training details on the ex-Pan Am aircraft taking about 1½hr each. The pilots are then type qualified and commence flying the routes with a training captain until fully experienced. A copilot would expect to be rated as a captain after about two years. For conversion to the K1, there are a further two 1½hr base training details to become accustomed to the different avionics fit, before achieving the type rating. The air-to-air refuelling training includes ground school lectures followed by flight training with receiver aircraft.

Above:
Little is changed for the pilots of the RAF TriStar from their civilian counterparts, apart from the addition of military equipment. *P. J. Birtles*

As part of the ongoing peacetime training programme, a typical sortie would be a 4½hr flight from Brize Norton to a special refuelling area at 25,000ft over the North Sea off Aberdeen. The purpose was to provide fuel for thirsty Phantoms of Nos 43 and 111 Squadrons and Tornado F3s from Nos 29 and 5 Squadrons.

The crew consisted of Flt Lt Ian Milton, with two co-pilots, Flt Lts Bill Austin and Tony Marshall, who shared the training detail. Master Engineer Bob Hall looked after the systems and was in overall control of refuelling and Master Air Loadmaster Michael Mead was responsible for the overall loading and centre of gravity of the aircraft, working closely with Bob Hall during the dispensing of the fuel. Ground Engineer, Chief Technician Ian Hunton was also on board, as he is responsible for the preparation of the aircraft for flight and any turnround servicing in the event of a landing away from base.

The fuel system on the Tristar can feed from any one tank into another, or any tank can feed into the hose for refuelling. For this particular sortie, ZD953 was loaded with 75 tonnes of fuel allowing up to 40 tonnes in the underfloor tanks.

However, for take-off and landing, during training flights, the underfloor tanks are kept empty to preserve the fatigue life of the aircraft. Obviously in an emergency this would not be a consideration.

At 11.20hr, the aircraft, call sign X5RO2, commenced engine start up off the APU in the order No 2, 1 and 3 and taxied for Runway 26 at Brize Norton at 11.28hr. Take-off was at 11.35hr with a lively climb out to cross airways at the Lichfield corridor at 18,000ft between Cosford and Northampton. Meanwhile, the fuselage tanks were loaded with 12 tonnes in the forward hold and 10 tonnes in the rear.

Once clear of the airways, the TriStar commenced climbing over the Yorkshire Moors to the planned height of 25,000ft, although refuelling can be achieved normally between 10,000ft and 35,000ft. The aircraft arrived on station at 12.20hr

and trailed the starboard hose and drogue at a
speed of 290kt (Mach 0.69). The 80ft of hose is
trailed, monitored by the Master Engineer
through the panel mounted video screen, the
camera being mounted in a rotating dome under
the rear fuselage of the aircraft. The camera can
cover in the horizontal plane the rear three
quarters of the aircraft from each engine and
main undercarriage, round to the other.

During the flight refuelling activities, the TriStar
captain is in overall charge of the operation. All
aircraft requiring fuel or any contact training,
whether planned or unplanned, make contact
with the tanker and formate on the port wingtip
until cleared by the captain to plug in. The initial
business on this occasion were four Phantoms of
No 43 Squadron which moved under the tail in
turn, making positive contact with the drogue by

pushing up 7ft to open the valve and receive fuel.
On completion, the aircraft pulls back slowly to
disconnect, and then formates on the starboard
side to await refuelling of any other aircraft. The
four Phantoms took on a total of about 11 tonnes
of fuel.

When the wet and dry contacts were completed
and the TriStar had dispensed all of its disposable
fuel, which amounted to 21 tonnes, before
leaving the training area, a practice intercept from
head on was flown. When the intercepting fighter
was about 11 miles in front of the tanker, the
TriStar was turned through 180°, and could either
be intercepted by the fighter on an offset track
equal to the diameter of the turn, or the TriStar
could return to the reciprocal of its original track.

With all tanking and training completed, the
return commenced to Brize Norton at 15.05hr,
cruising at 320kt/M 0.76, landing back on Runway 08 at 16.00hr, using remarkably little runway.

The TriStar has certainly brought an important
new capability to the RAF, and as the complete
fleet of aircraft are fully adapted to their intended
tasks, they will be able to play a major strategic
multi-role in the future defence of Great Britain.

12 TriStar Twilight

Since the completion of the writing of the first edition of this book in 1989, the TriStar has reached the twilight of its career, passing out of service with the original major trunk carriers (apart from two) and taking up operations with a number of smaller, mainly charter, airlines for long-range high-density services. The two major original operators of the TriStar which still have the aircraft in main line service are Delta Air Lines and Saudia, both of which have already placed orders for new generation aircraft to replace the now ageing wide-bodied trijet. The TriStar is still an effective and economical airliner but is becoming more maintenance intensive and parts for the once very advanced systems are becoming harder to obtain. However, Lockheed teamed with Delta, the largest remaining operator, to provide comprehensive support for the remaining aircraft in service. This combined the knowledge of the manufacturer with the unrivalled experience of an operator of the aircraft from first delivery in 1973, its fleet growing eventually to some 50 aircraft of all versions used both domestically and on international flights.

As well as charter operations, the TriStar is finding a useful niche with cargo operators, Marshall of Cambridge having established a good reputation for reconfigurations based on the knowledge gained with the tanker conversions for the RAF. Other adaptations of the TriStar have included a flying hospital and a satellite launcher.

In April 1989, Gulf Air, one of the early customers for the TriStar, ordered an additional six Boeing 767-300ERs, with some options, to start the replacement of the 11 TriStars of various marks, commencing with the withdrawal of the first two in June 1989. By mid-1992, Gulf Air still had eight TriStars in the fleet, due to the eco-

Below:
Gulf Air had its TriStars maintained by Marshall Aerospace at Cambridge, and as the aircraft were retired from service with the airline some were stored at Cambridge for eventual possible conversion to the cargo configuration. Gulf Air TriStar 200 A40-TW was later converted to a freighter for Arrow Air as N307GB.
Marshall of Cambridge Aerospace Ltd

nomic problems caused by the Gulf War. In 1997 Gulf Air was still experiencing economic problems and disposed of some of the 767s for much needed cash and brought out of storage three of the TriStars which it had been unable to sell.

By mid-1989 the TriStar was the mainstay of the AirLanka fleet with four in service and a further one due to be added. Sri Lanka is dependant upon tourism for its survival, and the destruction on the ground of a TriStar by a terrorist bomb, killing 16 passengers in 1986, was a major setback. In August 1991 the decision was made to replace the fleet of seven TriStars with five Airbus A340-300s starting in 1994.

Cathay Pacific was a major operator of the TriStar from its Hong Kong base on Asian regional services but placed orders for 10 Airbus A330-300s powered by Rolls-Royce RB211-524L engines in 1989 to eventually replace the fleet of TriStars. The Cathay fleet consisted of 14 TriStars with additions purchased from the bankrupt Eastern Airlines fleet. The aircraft were flying about 7hr a day due to restrictions with night time curfews at a number of airports in the region. The first of two Cathay TriStars was leased to Dragonair from 1 July 1990 for services to Shanghai and Beijing, eventually being replaced by A330s in May and September 1995. In mid-1990 Cathay announced that the by then 18-strong TriStar fleet had been sold to Airfleet Credit Finance, the

aircraft being withdrawn from 1995 onwards, as the A330s were delivered. After 21 years in service, Cathay operated the last TriStar revenue flight on 15 October 1996 between Nagoya and Taipei. The last flight was flown by VR-HHY which had been with the airline since 1978, had flown 39,754hr and made some 20,100 landings.

In June 1990 Air Canada also decided to sell its TriStar fleet, phasing out the eight L-1011-100s before the end of the year and replacing them with high-density Boeing 767s on leisure market routes. The remaining long-range TriStar 500s, which were used on international routes, were due to remain in service until being replaced by new 767-300ERs from 1993, but three were brought out of desert storage and painted in the new colours in mid-1994 to make up for a shortage in capacity.

By the end of 1990, a total of 237 TriStars were still in active service, with Delta and TWA in the USA operating fleets of 39 and 35 respectively, Caledonian Airways and LTU with five and

Above:
Faucett TriStar 1 OB-1545 seen on finals at Miami in January 1994. This aircraft made its first flight on 28 April 1974 and was delivered to TWA on 29 May as N31021. It was withdrawn from service in September 1992, and leased to Faucett on 25 August 1993.
Nick Granger

Below:
Delta Air Lines used the long range TriStar 500s for transatlantic services to Europe, but with the replacement of them by Boeing 767-300ERs, the TriStar 500s replaced some of the older versions on US domestic routes. Delta TriStar 500 N767DA is seen ready for departure at London Gatwick in May 1993. *Author*

10 respectively used for charter flights in Europe, Saudia with a fleet of 17 TriStar 200s and All Nippon Airways with 11 TriStar 1s used regionally from Tokyo. In early 1995 BA sold off its charter division, Caledonian Airways, to Inspirations. With the economic downturn caused by the Gulf War, a number of major airlines had to find ways of reducing costs. BA had already disposed of its TriStar 500s to the RAF for conversion to tankers, and decided to withdraw the nine TriStar 1s from service by the middle of 1990 due to a 20% fall in traffic. This left eight TriStar 200s in operation with the airline. However, by the end of 1991 the worldwide fleet of active TriStars had grown to 244, out of the original 250 built, as it still provided a very cost-effective means of air transport. One year later the fleet had begun the decline in numbers to 191 TriStars in airline service, with growing numbers arriving for desert storage. TWA had also filed for bankruptcy and submitted a recovery plan in early 1993 which involved the TriStar fleet declining to five aircraft by 1997, being counterbalanced by more modern and economic aircraft. In February 1996, TWA placed an order for 20 Boeing 757s, 15 being delivered by 1997 to replace the last of the TriStar fleet on US domestic routes.

The only major accident to a TriStar since 1989 was to TWA aircraft N11002 which caught fire during take-off from New York Kennedy on 30 July 1992. The take-off was abandoned and the aircraft turned off the runway on to soft ground, where the 274 passengers and 12 crew evacuated the aircraft safely before it burnt out completely. The cause of the accident was a combination of an incorrect stick shaker operation during rotation, followed by a crack in the rear spar caused by the overweight landing, spilling fuel from the integral tanks, which then ignited.

In March 1993 a major milestone was reached with the worldwide fleet of TriStars passing the 10 million flying-hours mark, the highest-time aircraft being with LTU which had logged 61,600hr since delivery in April 1980. The highest flight cycles had been achieved by an ANA TriStar, which had made 31,300 landings since delivery in July 1975. The majority of the fleet had reached the ageing airliner status, having been in operation for over 15 years, although the design life was well in excess of this.

By the end of 1993, Saudia was beginning to look at the long overdue requirement for the modernisation of the entire fleet, including the replacement of the TriStars as well as the Boeing

Below:
Due to financial difficulties BWIA was unable to replace the TriStar 500s used from the Caribbean to Europe as planned at the end of 1996. BWIA TriStar 500 9Y-TGN is seen ready for departure from London Heathrow in November 1996. *Author*

747-100s. The Boeing 777, Airbus A330/340 and MD-11 were all being considered. Delays were caused by economic difficulties within Saudi Arabia due to the large purchases of military aircraft, a contract for the new Boeing and McDonnell aircraft being signed in October 1995, with deliveries commencing in 1998, again with delays caused by financial problems.

As well as using the shorter-range TriStars domestically, Delta used the L-1011-500 for transatlantic flights to Gatwick, and then on to Frankfurt from November 1993, where a European hub had been established. This was achieved when Delta took over the PanAm routes in November 1991 with the demise of that airline, which also allowed the take over of a number of the old PanAm worldwide routes from Germany.

One of the well established TriStar 500 operators was BWIA International which operated four TriStars from the Caribbean to Europe but was beginning to look at replacing these aircraft in mid-1994. In November the Airbus A340 was selected to replace the TriStars, the first two scheduled originally to arrive towards the end of 1996. However, financial considerations delayed the confirmation of the order, keeping the TriStars in service longer than planned.

As mentioned earlier, Delta and Lockheed formed a strategic alliance to provide maintenance and technical support for the TriStar in December 1995, using the airline's Atlanta engineering base for light maintenance of the world fleet, with Lockheed Martin offering heavy maintenance at Greenville, North Carolina. However, Delta began the rundown of the TriStar fleet in February 1996 with further orders for 767-300ERs to replace the trijets on the North Atlantic routes, the long-range aircraft replacing earlier TriStars on domestic services. In 1997, Delta placed the launch order for the stretched Boeing 767-400ER, which finally decided the ultimate replacement for the TriStar with the airline.

TAP of Portugal was one of the last customers for the TriStar 500, having operated a fleet of five aircraft. While three of the aircraft were leased individually to LAM, TAAG and Air Mauritius, the final pair was sold to Air Transat, the Canadian charter operator, with delivery in January and February 1997.

With the merger of a number of the British charter airlines during the winter of 1998-9, including the demise of Caledonian Airways, the TriStar is less likely to be seen flying around Europe, especially as some are reaching the end of their economic lives. A number of the aircraft have been broken up for spares at Hurn and Bruntingthorpe as well as in North America. The conversion of more modern aircraft like the Airbus A300 and the Boeing 767 may also reduce the market for further cargo conversions of the Tristar.

Below:
TAP Air Portugal was one of the last customers for the TriStar, operating a fleet of five aircraft. Three have been leased to other operators, while the remaining two were delivered to Air Transat in early 1997. TAP Air Portugal TriStar 500 CS-TEE is seen on final approach to London Heathrow in May 1992 and was one of the two sold to Air Transat. *Author*

Above:
Linhas Aéreas de Moçambique (LAM) TriStar 500 CS-TEA on lease from TAP, seen on arrival at Gatwick in June 1996. This aircraft was originally delivered to TAP on 5 January 1983. *Nick Granger*

Below:
TradeWinds TriStar 1 N826CR at Gatwick in May 1998 operating a Britannia charter. Originally delivered to Eastern as N334EA in November 1976, this aircraft was acquired by Delta in July 1991 as N788DL. *Nick Granger*

Above

TriStar 150 C-FTNA was originally in service with Air Canada, but was sold to Air Transat for charter operations across the North Atlantic. Air Transat TriStar C-FTNA is seen ready for departure from London Gatwick in August 1995. *Author*

Above right:

Royal Jordanian was one of the later customers for the TriStar 500, and an additional aircraft was purchased for the Jordanian Royal Flight. Carrying the basic airline colours, the aircraft JY-HKJ carries the title of 'The Hashemite Kingdom of Jordan' and is maintained by Marshall Aerospace. *Marshall of Cambridge Aerospace Ltd*

Centre right:

Nordic East TriStar 1 SE-DTC operated on holiday charter flights from Sweden, is seen at Rhodes in September 1995. It was sold to Blue Scandinavia at the end of the 1996 season. *Author*

Below:

Rich International TriStar 1 N302MB at Gatwick in August 1995. This aircraft was originally delivered to ANA as JA8518 on 19 April 1976. It was withdrawn from service on 17 November 1993 and acquired by Rich a year later. *Nick Granger*

Below right:

Blue Scandinavia commenced operations with TriStar 1 SE-DTC to the Greek holiday resorts in 1997, as well as using a Boeing 757. The airline was taken over by Britannia Airways at the beginning of 1998. *Göran Håkansson*

Above

Peach Air also operates standby TriStars from Gatwick to help provide an increased capacity. Peach Air TriStar 1 TF-ABE is seen at Rhodes in August 1997 operating a Caledonian service; it was previously N314EA with Eastern Airlines. *Author*

Below:

TriStar 100 G-BBAF on lease to Aer Lingus from Caledonian Airways at Gatwick in September 1997. This aircraft made its first flight on 14 October 1974 and was delivered to BA on 8 November, moving to Caledonian in December 1990. *Nick Granger*

Bottom:

As well as operating a fleet of TriStar 200s, Saudia also operates, on behalf of the Saudi Royal Flight, TriStar 500 HZ-HM5. This is the 250th and last TriStar built, and was originally ordered by the Algerian VIP Flight, but never confirmed. It is one of two TriStar 500s used by the Saudi Royal Flight. *Marshall of Cambridge Aerospace Ltd*

TriStar Conversions

Although Marshall of Cambridge is the acknowledged expert in TriStar conversions, in particular to the cargo configuration following the modifications for the RAF, there was reported to be one unsuccessful attempt to make a cargo conversion in the USA, which was to be delivered to Southern World Airlines in New Zealand. However, it does not appear to have entered operation due to certification problems, and the aircraft identity cannot be confirmed.

In March 1991 Saudia was having discussions with the Lockheed Commercial Aircraft Centre about the conversion of their TriStar fleet to cargo aircraft, while Pemco was also hoping to proceed on a major conversion programme for an unnamed customer which was delayed due to uncertainty caused by the Gulf situation. Wide-bodied aircraft had proved difficult to convert to economic freighters, because the cross section beam strength with the large cut-out of the cargo door is difficult to achieve without incurring unacceptable weight penalties. The floor strengthening and loading systems also add further weight.

In July 1992 Lockheed Aircraft Services (LAS) announced the launch of the Lockheed 2000 freighter conversion, to be fitted with a 4.3m by 2.9m upward opening cargo door on the port side of the forward cabin. The aircraft was expected to carry a payload of some 55,400kg over distances of around 4,600km (2,500nm) and the major conversion work was to be done at the Lockheed Aeromod Center in Tucson, with Lockheed Aeronautical Systems of Marietta providing technical support to provide optional increases in take-off weight, landing weight, zero fuel weight, range and payload up to 69,900kg. LAS had contemplated working with Marshall Aerospace, but rejected it, as the earlier military conversion was claimed not to be cost-effective for commercial applications, although Marshall had worked closely with Lockheed for the vital design data. Avtec of Basle was appointed as marketing partner. The Marshall design had proposed a maximum payload of between 51,300 and 66,500kg loaded through a 2.6m by 3.5m cargo door.

Marshall Aerospace was however not discouraged and confirmed in August 1992 that it was still offering cargo conversions of the TriStar, although the door size had been increased to 2.9m by 3.9m. In an agreement with Lockheed Aeronautical Systems (LASC), which had approved the original RAF conversions by Marshall, LASC would publish a service bulletin covering the work, although at the time no confirmed orders had been placed. Despite some encouraging interest for the conversion of up to 15 aircraft by LAS, no orders were placed, and the Lockheed-based TriStar freighter programme never started.

Marshall Aerospace was however more suc-

Below:
The civil cargo conversion programme at Marshall Aerospace was launched by an order from American International Airways. The first aircraft was converted from an ex-BA TriStar 200 G-BHBM, making its first flight from Cambridge on 11 August 1995 and being delivered five days later.
Marshall of Cambridge Aerospace Ltd

cessful using the TriStar 200 as a basis for conversion, increasing the maximum gross take-off weight from 212,000kg to 215,000kg. The cargo capacity consisted of up to 23 2.25m by 3.2m pallets on the main deck, with 16 LD-3 containers up to a weight of 16,400kg in the forward underfloor hold, and a further eight containers in the rear underfloor hold carrying up to a weight of 8,200kg. Marshall has the manufacturing capability to complete up to three cargo conversions at a time, with any additional capacity being passed to Lockheed Martin in Greenville,

Above:
AIA also acquired TriStar 200 N108CK on 31 July 1995 and retained the passenger configuration for charter flights. Seen at Gatwick in May 1997 operating for Airtours, this aircraft was originally delivered to BA on 1 April 1981 as G-BHBN, and was withdrawn from service with the airline in June 1991. *Nick Granger*

Below:
Miami-based Arrow Air leased three ex-Gulf Air TriStar 200 freighter conversions from IAL in early 1995. N306GB was previously A40-TY with Gulf Air.
Marshall of Cambridge Aerospace Ltd

which has the capacity for the conversion of two further aircraft.

The Marshall civil cargo conversion of TriStars was launched by an order for three conversions from American International Airways (AIA) in July 1994, with options on a further five. A batch of ex-British Airways TriStar 200s were allocated to this programme and by the end of 1996, 12 aircraft had either been converted, and had entered service, or were in the conversion programme. In early 1995 International Air Leases (IAL) placed an order for three conversions of ex-Gulf Air TriStar 200s for operation by Miami-based Arrow Air, and a further conversation of an ex-LTU L-1011-200 was ordered by ILFC for Millon Air, also based at Miami.

The first civil freighter made its maiden flight from Cambridge on 11 August 1995, and was handed over to Mr Connie Kalitta, President of AIA, on 16 August as N102CK. Although the initial conversion had taken some 14 months, Marshall planned to reduce the work period to between three and four months, depending upon the customer specification and any additional work required to bring the aircraft up to date with modifications and service bulletins. The first aircraft entered service during mid-September operating services on behalf of Millon Air to South American destinations.

The major change in the conversion programme, compared with the modifications for the RAF, was to support the airframe neutrally and build the cargo door surround directly into the airframe, before introducing the British Aerospace Aerostructures Manchester-built cargo door. In the case of the military conversions, the door surround had been jig built separately, and then installed into the structure. Marshall Aerospace has therefore successfully overcome the difficulties of producing an economic wide-bodied cargo conversion capable of carrying significant loads over medium and long ranges.

An unusual TriStar conversion, also undertaken by Marshall Aerospace, was the launch vehicle for the Orbital Sciences Pegasus Satellite booster. The former Air Canada TriStar 1-15 was delivered to Cambridge in June 1992 for the modification programme to commence, and due for flight test in the first quarter of 1993. Pegasus had previously been launched from under the wing of a NASA B-52, but in the case of the TriStar conversion the booster was mounted under the fuselage. Provision was made in the TriStar conversion for the launch of the 23,587kg Pegasus XL, 4,535kg heavier than the original model. The lower galley was removed, much of the cabin stripped out of its passenger configuration, and the doors no longer required were sealed permanently. The booster support system was built into wingbox centre section between the first and third spars, which was not

Below:
LTU TriStar 200 D-AERN was converted to the cargo configuration by Marshall Aerospace for ILFC, which leased the aircraft registered N851MA to Miami-based Millon Air.
Marshall of Cambridge Aerospace Ltd

used for fuel in that version. The Pegasus airframe has high stub wings, anhedral tailplane and the fin recessed into the underside of the TriStar fuselage.

The modified aircraft made its maiden flight from Cambridge on 12 July 1993, and on the sixth flight about one month later carried a dummy Pegasus weighing 23,500kg for the first time. The three-stage Pegasus satellite launch vehicle is capable of carrying satellites up to 650km into orbit at considerably reduced cost compared with normal rocket launches. The first successful powered launch of a Pegasus was made on 3 April 1995, the normal launch altitude being around 38,000ft.

Another interesting conversion, this time not by Marshall Aerospace, was that of an ex-PSA TriStar into a flying hospital. First announced in July 1995, the conversion was undertaken by Lockheed Martin Aircraft Services for Operation Blessing International Relief and Development. In the $14.5 million contract, the TriStar is the largest self-contained hospital aircraft ever built. The main deck has been fitted out with an operating theatre, a pre/post operation section, surgical preparation area and patient examination area. In addition the main deck also houses two dental and an ear/nose/ throat treatment surgeries. The lower deck, which is reached by the

special door provided for PSA for a lower cabin entry, is fitted with a pharmacy and a check in/check out reception, while the galley and crew rest area doubles as a consulting room. The aircraft is designed to operate independently on station in Third World countries for a week at a time and is fitted with auxiliary ground power generators and water purification system, the overall conversion being completed by June 1996.

When the Flying Hospital visited the Farnborough Air Show in September 1998, a total of seven medical missions had already been completed to a number of countries including El Salvador, the Ukraine, Brazil and Bolivia, with missions planned to India and Nicaragua before the end of the year. In addition to helping to cure sick people in these countries, the medical team helps train local medics to carry on the work of the Flying Hospital after it has departed.

Below:
Converted by Lockheed Martin Aircraft Services for Operation Blessing, TriStar 100 N787M was originally delivered to PSA as N10112. Now equipped as The Flying Hospital, the aircraft is used to provide medical assistance and training to Third World countries.
The Flying Hospital

RAF Operations

Since the original introduction into service, some changes have been made in the operation of TriStars with the RAF, and three different configurations are used in the fleet of nine aircraft with No 216 Squadron based at Lyneham. Six of the TriStars, as earlier mentioned, were ex-BA TriStar 500s, two being configured as tanker/passenger transport aircraft with the designation K.Mk1s, without the main deck cargo doors, and with 196 seats. The other four ex-BA aircraft are to the full tanker/transport standard as KC.Mk1s with the cargo door on the main deck. The interior is mounted on pallets, whether it is cargo or seats or a combination of both. When seats are loaded, galleys are also fitted on pallets and as the underfloor holds are full with the extra fuel tanks, the passengers baggage is loaded on the main deck on pallets. The three ex-PanAm TriStar 500s have been retained as C.Mk2s without cargo doors or tanker modifications and are capable of carrying up to 250 passengers.

The RAF TriStars played a major support role in the Gulf War, the K.1s flying over 90 air-to-air refuelling missions totalling over 430hr, the other TriStars in the fleet providing flight refuelling support for aircraft deploying to the Gulf, as well as transporting troops and equipment. None of the RAF TriStars has retained the flight refuelling probe above the cockpit, as not only does the aircraft carry more than enough fuel internally for all normal operations, but the modern large fan engines do not perform well with rapid changes of power when trying to approach a drogue, and the large momentum of the aircraft is also difficult to control in close formation. The four KC.Mk1s are used regularly on flight refuelling sorties from Brize Norton, the main training area being just off the east coast of Britain from the Wash to the north of Scotland. One of the operational changes from when the TriStars were first introduced is that the aircraft requiring fuel now approach from the starboard side and wait their turn, formating on the port side when completed, if part of a formation group, or just departing if operating singly. Although most of the trade are the fast jets, VC-10s are about the largest aircraft to take on fuel.

Left:
TriStar KC.1 ZD953 of No 216 Squadron trailing a hose is being approached by a VC-10 (out of the picture) of Nos 10 Squadron on the starboard side of the TriStar, ready to take on fuel. *Author*

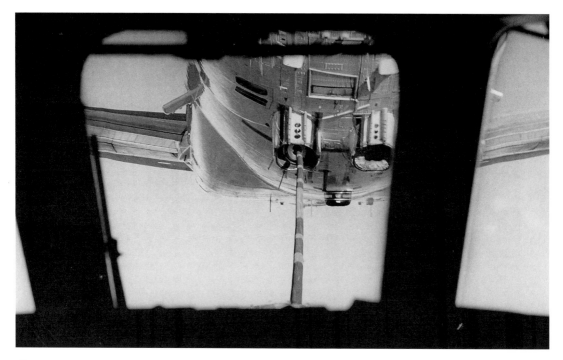

The VC-10 of No 10 Squadron linked up to the left hand HDU on No 216 Squadron TriStar ZD953. Two HDUs (hose drive units) are provided in case of unservicability of one. The momentum of the large VC-10 made formating on the drogue very difficult. *Author*

The interior of the No 216 Squadron TriStar KC.1s can be fitted out with seats on pallets, including a galley unit, and room for cargo and baggage by the large cargo door. There is a limitation on use of the rear toilets during flight refuelling, as if the wash basin is drained, the water is discharged overboard, forming ice and hitting the aircraft behind. *Author*

Above:
TriStar KC.1 ZD953 of No 216 Squadron being prepared for its next sortie from Brize Norton with the upward opening cargo door open. *Author*

Below:
The normal trade for the No 216 squadron TriStar KC.1s are NATO fast jets. The TriStar is seen here refuelling a Tornado F3 of No 29 Squadron, with Tornado F3s of Nos 25 and 43 Squadrons waiting their turn. *RAF*

Appendices

Lockheed-California
PO Box 551, 2555N Hollywood Way
Burbank, California 91520
USA

1 Lockheed 1011 TriStar Specification

	L-1011-1	L-1011-100	L-1011-200	L-1011-250	L-1011-500
Power plant	3RR RB211-22B	3RR RB211-22B	3RR RB211-524B	3RR RB211-524B	3RR RB211-524B
Thrust (lb)	42,000	42,000	50,000	50,000	50,000
Wing span	155ft 4in	155ft 4in	155ft 4in	155ft 4in	164ft 4in
Length	177ft 8in	177ft 8in	177ft 8in	177ft 8in	164ft 2in
Height	55ft 4in	55ft 4in	55ft 4in	55ft 4in	55ft 4in
Wing area (ft^2)	3,456	3,456	3,456	3,456	3,540
Wing sweep (¼-chord)	35°	35°	35°	35°	35°
Maximum seating	400	400	400	400	330
Cargo volume (ft^3)	3,900	3,900	3,900	3,900	4,235
Take-off weight (lb)	430,000	466,000	466,000	510,000	496,000
Landing weight (lb)	358,000	368,000	368,000	368,000	368,000
Fuel contents (Imp gal)	19,636	21,998	21,998	26,347	26,347
Max cruise speed (kt) at 33,000ft	512	512	518	518	518
Max payload (lb)/ range (nm)	83,270/2,950	73,534/4,030	71,415/4,260	88,240/4,850	92,253/4,580

2 TriStar Production

C/N	Registration initial	Registration current	Series	Current Operator	Fleet No/Name	Remarks
1001	N1011	—	1	Lockheed	—	BU for spares
1002	N31001	N301EA	1	Eastern	301	—
1003	N301EA	N302EA	1	Eastern	302	—
1004	N302EA	N303EA	1	Eastern	303	—
1005	N6752	N304EA	1	Eastern	304	WFU 16/01/84
1006	N303EA	N305EA	1	Eastern	305	—
1007	N306EA	—	1	Eastern	306	WFU 30/01/84
1008	N307EA	D-AERY	1	LTU	—	—
1009	N308EA	—	1	Eastern	308	—
1010	N309EA	—	1	Eastern	309	—
1011	N310EA	—	1	Eastern	310	W/O 29/12/72
1012	N311EA	—	1	Eastern	311	WFU 22/05/85
1013	N31001	—	1	TWA	11001	—
1014	N11002	—	1	TWA	11002	—
1015	N11003	—	1	TWA	11003	—
1016	N11004	—	1	TWA	11004	—
1017	N11005	—	1	TWA	11005	—
1018	N11006	—	1	TWA	11006	—
1019	N312EA	C-FTNA	1	Air Canada	501	—
1020	N313EA	—	1	Eastern	313	—
1021	C-FTNB	—	1	Air Canada	502	—
1022	N314EA	—	1	Eastern	314	—
1023	N315EA	C-FTNC	1	Air Canada	503	—
1024	G-BAAA	VR-HHV	1	Cathay Pacific	—	Ex-Court Line
1025	CF-TND	A40-TP	1	Gulf Air	—	—

C/N	Registration initial	Registration current	Series	Current Operator	Fleet No/Name	Remarks
1026	N31007	—	1	TWA	11007	W/O 20/04/74
1027	C-FTNE	—	1	Air Canada	505	—
1028	N31008	—	1	TWA	11008	—
1029	N31009	—	1	TWA	11009	—
1030	N31010	—	1	TWA	11010	—
1031	N31011	—	1	TWA	11011	—
1032	G-BAAB	VR-HHW	1	Cathay Pacific	—	Ex-Court Line
1033	D-AERA	N372EA	1	Eastern	372	Ex-LTU
1034	N31012	N41012	1	TWA	11012	—
1035	N31013	—	1	TWA	11013	—
1036	N31014	—	1	TWA	11014	—
1037	N316EA	—	1	Eastern	316	—
1038	N317EA	—	1	Eastern	317	—
1039	N318EA	—	1	Eastern	318	—
1040	N319EA	—	1	Eastern	319	—
1041	N701DA	N701TT	50	Total Air/Air America	—	Ex-Delta
1042	N320EA	—	1	Eastern	320	—
1043	N321EA	—	1	Eastern	321	—
1044	N322EA	—	1	Eastern	322	—
1045	N323EA	—	1	Eastern	323	—
1046	N702DA	N702TT	50	Total Air/Air America	—	Ex-Delta
1047	G-FTNF	A40-TR	1	Gulf Air	–	Ex-Air Canada
1048	C-FTNG	—	1	Air Canada	507	—
1049	C-FTNH	—	1	Air Canada	508	—
1050	N324EA	—	1	Eastern	324	—
1051	N325EA	VR-HHY	1	Cathay Pacific	—	Ex-Eastern
1052	N703DA	N185AT	1	American Transair	185	—
1053	JA8501	4R-ULC	100	Air Lanka	City of Jayawardanapura	Ex-ANA
1054	N326EA	VR-HHX	1	Cathay Pacific	—	—
1055	N327EA	—	1	Eastern	327	—
1056	N328EA	A40-TV	100	Gulf Air	—	Ex-Eastern
1057	N704DA	N192AT	1	American Transair	192	Ex-Delta
1058	N64854	C-FTNI	100	Air Canada	509	—
1059	N31015	—	1	TWA	11015	—
1060	N31016	N41016	1	TWA	11016	—
1061	JA8502	4R-ULD	100	Air Lanka	—	W/O 03/05/86
1062	JA8503	4R-ULE	200	Air Lanka	City of Ratnapura	Ex-ANA
1063	N15017	—	1	TWA	11017	—
1064	N10112	C-GIES	100	Worldways	101	Ex-PSA
1065	N31018	—	50	TWA	21018	—
1066	N31019	—	50	TWA	21019	—
1067	N64854	C-FTNJ	100	Air Canada	510	—
1068	JA8505	A40-TS	1	Gulf Air	—	Ex-ANA
1069	N64854	C-FTNK	1	Air Canada	511	—
1070	JA8506	N762BE	50	Hawaiian Air	Waikiki	Ex-ANA
1071	N705DA	N193AT	1	American Transair	193	Ex-Delta
1072	N41020	—	50	TWA	21020	—
1073	N64854	C-FTNL	100	Air Canada	512	—
1074	N706DA	N186AT	1	Air Algerie lease	—	Ex-Delta
1075	N31021	—	50	TWA	21021	—
1076	N31022	—	50	TWA	21022	—
1077	N707DA	N187AT	1	American Transair	187	Ex-Delta
1078	N708DA	N188AT	1	American Transair	188	Ex-Delta
1079	N10114	C-G1FE	100	Worldways	102	Ex-PSA
1080	N31023	—	50	TWA	21023	—
1081	N709DA	N189AT	1	American Transair	189	Ex-Delta
1082	JA8507	N763BE	50	Hawaiian Air	Maui	Ex-ANA
1083	N64854	G-BBAE	1	BA	Torbay	—
1084	N710DA	N191AT	1	American Transair	191	Ex-Delta
1085	N329EA	—	1	Eastern	329	—

C/N	Registration initial	Registration current	Series	Current Operator	Fleet No/Name	Remarks
1086	N711DA	N190AT	1	American Transair	190	Ex-Delta
1087	N330EA	—	1	Eastern	330	—
1088	N712DA	—	1	Delta	712	—
1089	N713DA	—	1	Delta	713	—
1090	N714DA	—	1	Delta	714	—
1091	N31024	—	50	TWA	21024	—
1092	N715DA	—	1	Delta	715	—
1093	G-BBAF	—	1	BA	*Babbacombe Bay*	—
1094	G-BBAG	—	1	BA	*Bridgewater Bay*	—
1095	N716DA	—	1	Delta	716	—
1096	N717DA	—	1	Delta	717	—
1097	N718DA	—	1	Delta	718	—
1098	N80125	—	100	TWA	31025	—
1099	JA8508	—	1	All-Nippon	—	—
1100	JA8509	—	1	All-Nippon	—	—
1101	G-BBAH	—	1	BA	*Lyme Bay*	—
1102	G-BBAI	—	1	BA	*St Brides Bay*	—
1103	JA8510	N703TT	50	Total Air/Air America	—	Ex-ANA
1104	N81026	—	100	TWA	31026	—
1105	JA8511	N765BE	50	Hawaiian	*Kauai*	Ex-ANA
1106	G-BBAJ	—	1	BA	*Elizabeth Harkness Rose*	—
1107	N81027	—	50	TWA	21027	—
1108	N81028	—	100	TWA	31028	—
1109	N31029	—	100	TWA	31029	—
1110	N64854	HZ-AHA	200	Saudia	—	—
1111	N31030	—	100	TWA	31030	—
1112	JA8512	N766BE	50	Hawaiian	*Oahu*	Ex-ANA
1113	JA8513	N764BE	50	Hawaiian	*Wahwaii*	Ex-ANA
1114	N10115	D-AERI	1	LTU	—	Ex-PSA
1115	N31031	—	100	TWA	31031	—
1116	HZ-AHB	—	200	Saudia	—	—
1117	JA8514	—	1	All-Nippon	—	—
1118	N64854	VR-HHK	100	Cathay Pacific	—	—
1119	JA8515	—	1	All-Nippon	—	—
1120	N10116	D-AERE	1	LTU	—	Ex-PSA
1121	N48354	N331EA	1	Eastern	331	—
1122	VR-HHL	—	100	Cathay Pacific	—	—
1123	N332EA	—	1	Eastern	332	—
1124	N31032	HZ-AHE	200	Saudia	—	Ex-TWA
1125	N10117	D-AERU	1	LTU	—	Ex-PSA
1126	N333EA	—	1	Eastern	333	—
1127	JA8516	—	1	All-Nippon	—	—
1128	JA8517	—	1	All-Nippon	—	—
1129	JA8518	—	1	All-Nippon	—	—
1130	N31033	HZ-AHF	200	Saudia	—	Ex-TWA
1131	G-BDCW	A40-TW	200	Gulf Air	—	—
1132	G-BEAK	—	50	BA	*Carmarthen Bay*	—
1133	G-BDCX	A40-TX	200	Gulf Air	—	—
1134	JA8519	—	1	All-Nippon	—	—
1135	N719DA	—	1	Delta	719	—
1136	N720DA	—	1	Delta	720	—
1137	HZ-AHC	—	200	Saudia	—	—
1138	G-BDCY	A40-TY	200	Gulf Air	—	—
1139	N721DA	—	1	Delta	721	—
1140	G-BDCZ	A40-TZ	200	Gulf Air	—	—
1141	N334EA	—	1	Eastern	334	—
1142	N335EA	—	1	Eastern	335	—
1143	N336EA	—	1	Eastern	336	—
1144	N48354	HZ-AHD	200	Saudia	—	—
1145	G-BEAL	—	50	BA	*Cardigan Bay*	—

C/N	Registration initial	Registration current	Series	Current Operator	Fleet No/Name	Remarks
1146	G-BEAM	—	50	BA	*Swansea Bay*	—
1147	N722DA	—	1	Delta	722	—
1148	HZ-AHG	—	200	Saudia	—	—
1149	HZ-AHH	—	200	Saudia	—	—
1150	N723DA	—	1	Delta	723	—
1151	N724DA	—	200	Delta	724	—
1152	N337EA	D-AERP	1	LTU	—	Ex-Eastern
1153	N338EA	D-AERM	1	LTU	—	Ex-Eastern
1154	JA8520	—	1	All-Nippon	—	—
1155	JA8521	—	1	All-Nippon	—	—
1156	JA8522	—	1	All-Nippon	—	—
1157	G-BFCA	ZD948	500	RAF	216 Squadron	Ex-BA
1158	N339EA	D-AERN	1	LTU	—	Ex-Eastern
1159	G-BFCB	ZD949	500	RAF	216 Squadron	Ex-BA
1160	HZ-AHI	—	200	Saudia	—	—
1161	HZ-AHJ	—	200	Saudia	—	—
1162	N725DA	—	1	Delta	725	—
1163	N726DA	—	1	Delta	726	W/O 02/08/85
1164	G-BFCC	ZD950	500	RAF	216 Squadron	Ex-BA
1165	G-BFCD	ZD951	500	RAF	216 Squadron	Ex-BA
1166	N751DA	—	500	Delta	751	—
1167	N727DA	—	1	Delta	727	—
1168	G-BFCE	ZD952	500	RAF	216 Squadron	Ex-BA
1169	HZ-AHK	—	200	Saudia	—	W/O 14/08/80
1170	HZ-AHL	—	200	Saudia	—	—
1171	HZ-AHM	—	200	Saudia	—	—
1172	N752DA	—	500	Delta	752	—
1173	N728DA	—	1	Delta	728	—
1174	G-BFCF	ZD953	500	RAF	216 Squadron	Ex-BA
1175	HZ-AHN	—	200	Saudia	—	—
1176	N64911	N501PA	500	United	1001	Ex- Pan Am
1177	N503PA	ZE706	500	RAF	216 Squadron	Ex-Pan Am
1178	G-BGBB	—	200	BA	*Bridlington Bay*	—
1179	9Y-TGJ	—	500	BWIA	595 *Flamingo*	—
1180	N729DA	—	1	Delta	729	—
1181	N504PA	N754DA	500	Delta	754	Ex-Pan Am
1182	G-BGBC	—	200	BA	*St Andrews Bay*	—
1183	D-AERT	—	500	LTU	—	—
1184	N505PA	N755DL	500	Delta	755	Ex-Pan Am
1185	N507PA	N756DR	500	Delta	756	Ex-Pan Am
1186	N508PA	ZE704	500	RAF	216 Squadron	Ex-Pan Am
1187	HZ-AHO	—	200	Saudia	—	—
1188	N509PA	ZE705	500	RAF	216 Squadron	Ex-Pan Am
1189	N753DA	—	500	Delta	753	—
1190	HZ-AHP	—	200	Saudia	—	—
1191	9Y-TGN	—	500	BWIA	596	—
1192	HZ-AHQ	—	200	Saudia	—	—
1193	G-BHBL	—	200	BA	*Largo Bay*	—
1194	N4003G	N510PA	500	United	1010	Ex-Pan Am
1195	N511PA	—	500	United	1011	Ex-Pan Am
1196	D-AERL	—	500	LTU	—	—
1197	N512PA	—	500	United	1012	Ex-Pan Am
1198	G-BHBM	—	200	BA	*Poole Bay*	—
1199	N730DA	—	1	Delta	730	—
1200	N1731D	—	1	Delta	731	—
1201	N92TA	—	200	Gulf Air	—	—
1202	C-GAGF	—	500	Air Canada	551	—
1203	N92TB	—	200	Gulf Air	—	—
1204	G-BHBN	—	200	BA	*Bideford Bay*	—
1205	G-BHBO	—	200	BA	*St Magnus Bay*	—

C/N	Registration initial	Registration current	Series	Current Operator	Fleet No/Name	Remarks
1206	G-GAGG	—	500	Air Canada	552	—
1207	C-GAGH	—	500	Air Canada	553	—
1208	N513PA	—	500	United	1013	Ex-Pan Am
1209	C-GAGI	—	500	Air Canada	554	—
1210	N514PA	—	500	United	1014	Ex-Pan Am
1211	G-BHBP	—	200	BA	*Whitsand Bay*	—
1212	G-BHBR	—	200	BA	*Bude Bay*	—
1213	N1732D	—	1	Delta	732	—
1214	HZ-AHR	—	200	Saudia	—	—
1215	N31032	—	100	TWA	31032	—
1216	N4009G	C-GAGJ	500	Air Canada	555	—
1217	JY-AGA	—	500	Alia	*Abas Ibn Firnas*	—
1218	C-GAGK	—	500	Air Canada	556	—
1219	JY-AGB	—	500	Alia	*Ibn Battouta*	—
1220	JY-AGC	—	500	Alia	*Al-Jawaheri*	—
1221	N31033	—	100	TWA	31033	—
1222	9Y-THA	—	500	BWIA	597	—
1223	A40-TT	—	200	Gulf Air	107	—
1224	N733DS	—	1	Delta	733	—
1225	N1734D	—	1	Delta	734	—
1226	N735D	—	1	Delta	735	—
1227	N736DY	—	1	Delta	736	—
1228	N737D	—	1	Delta	737	—
1229	JY-AGD	—	500	Alia	*Ibn Sina*	—
1230	N8034T	—	100	TWA	31034	—
1231	N7035T	—	100	TWA	31035	—
1232	N7036T	—	100	TWA	31036	—
1233	9Y-THB	N3140D	500	BWIA	598	—
1234	N1738D	—	250	Delta	738	—
1235	4R-ULA	G-BLUS	500	Air Lanka	*Laggan Bay*	Leased to BA
1236	4R-ULB	G-BLUT	500	Air Lanka	*Dunnet Bay*	Leased to BA
1237	N1739D	—	250	Delta	739	—
1238	JY-AGE	—	500	Alia	*Al Biruni*	—
1239	CS-TEA	—	500	TAP	*Luis de Carnões*	—
1240	CS-TEB	—	500	TAP	*Infante D. Henrique*	—
1241	CS-TEC	—	500	TAP	*Cago Coutinho*	—
1242	CS-TED	—	500	TAP	*Bartolomeu de Gusmão*	—
1243	CS-TEE	—	500	TAP	*St António de Lisboa*	—
1244	N740DA	—	1	Delta	740	—
1245	N741DA	—	1	Delta	741	—
1246	N64959	JY-AGI	500	Alia	—	—
1247	JY-HKJ	—	500	Jordan Royal Flight	—	—
1248	JY-AGJ	—	500	Alia	—	—
1249	JY-AGH	—	500	Alia	—	—
1250	7T-VRA	—	500	Algeria VIP Flight	—	Not delivered